Absence

Byung-Chul Han

Absence

On the Culture and Philosophy
of the Far East

Translated by Daniel Steuer

polity

Originally published in German as *Abwesen: Zur Kultur und Philosophie des fernen Ostens* © Merve Verlag, 2007

This English edition © Polity Press, 2023

Excerpt from *Berlin Childhood around 1900* by Walter Benjamin, translated by Howard Eiland, Cambridge, MA: The Belknap Press of Harvard University Press, Copyright © 2006 by the President and Fellows of Harvard College. Used by permission. All rights reserved.

Excerpt from *Phantasien der Wiederholung* by Peter Handke © Suhrkamp Verlag Frankfurt am Main 1983. All rights reserved by and controlled through Suhrkamp Verlag Berlin.

Excerpt from *Silence: Lectures and Writings* © 1961 by John Cage, page 191. Published by Wesleyan University Press. Used by permission.

Polity Press
65 Bridge Street
Cambridge CB2 1UR, UK

Polity Press
111 River Street
Hoboken, NJ 07030, USA

ISBN-13: 978-1-5095-4619-0 – hardback
ISBN-13: 978-1-5095-4620-6 – paperback

A catalogue record for this book is available from the British Library.

Library of Congress Control Number: 2022945469

Typeset in 10.75 on 14pt Janson Text
by Cheshire Typesetting Ltd, Cuddington, Cheshire
Printed and bound in Great Britain by TJ Books Ltd, Padstow, Cornwall

The publisher has used its best endeavours to ensure that the URLs for external websites referred to in this book are correct and active at the time of going to press. However, the publisher has no responsibility for the websites and can make no guarantee that a site will remain live or that the content is or will remain appropriate.

Every effort has been made to trace all copyright holders, but if any have been overlooked the publisher will be pleased to include any necessary credits in any subsequent reprint or edition.

For further information on Polity, visit our website:
politybooks.com

The story comes from China, and tells of an old painter who invited friends to see his newest picture. This picture showed a park and a narrow footpath that ran along a stream and through a grove of trees, culminating at the door of a little cottage in the background. When the painter's friends, however, looked around for the painter, they saw that he was gone – that he was in the picture. There, he followed the little path that led to the door, paused before it quite still, turned, smiled, and disappeared through the narrow opening.

Walter Benjamin, *Berlin Childhood around 1900*[1]

CONTENTS

LIST OF ILLUSTRATIONS

PREFACE

For a long time, the West either violently excluded or appropriated the foreign. The foreign had no presence within what was proper to the West. And today? Is there still something like the foreign? It is currently fashionable to believe that everyone is somehow like everyone else. In this way, the foreign again disappears from what is considered as proper to the West. Maybe it would not be a disadvantage to believe that there is a country 'where anyone who says "I" is immediately swallowed up by the earth'.[1] It is salutary to maintain a space for the foreign. It is an expression of friendliness that makes it possible to become *other to oneself*. This book presents a *foreign* culture, a culture of *absencing* that will appear rather astounding to the inhabitants of the occidental culture, which is centred on essence.

Essencing and Absencing
– Living Nowhere

A good wanderer leaves no trace.[1]
Laozi, *Daodejing*

The original meanings of the German word 'Wesen' (Old High German *wesan*) [essence], interestingly, were 'to linger in one place', 'stay', 'household matters', 'dwelling' and 'duration'. Vesta, the Roman goddess of the hearth, home and family, has the same etymological root. Essence refers to house and household, to ownership and property, to what endures and is solid. Essence is *abode*. The house shelters possessions and belongings. The inwardness of the house is inherent in essence. The Greek word 'ousia', which Aristotle uses for 'essence', also originally means property, estate [Anwesen] and land holdings. The concept of 'essence', which unites identity, duration and inwardness, dwelling, lingering and possessing, dominates occidental metaphysics. For Plato, the beautiful is the identical, the unchanging, the enduring. It is 'itself by itself with itself, it is always one in form'.[2] Plato's

1

Eros, who strives for divine beauty, is the son of Poros. The plural form of Poros also means intake and money. Poros, literally 'the way', is meant to lead to possession. This goal-directed way is fully absorbed by the intention to possess. When it does not lead to *unambiguous* possession, the situation becomes *a-poretic*. Because of his father, Plato says, Eros is himself an 'awesome hunter'.[3] Power and possession animate him. Being, to him, means *desire*.

Essence is substance. It subsists. It is the unchanging that withstands change by persisting in itself as itself and thereby differs from everything else. The Latin verb *substare*, from which 'substance' is derived, means among other things 'withstand'. And *stare* is also used in the sense of 'to assert one-self'. On the strength of its substantiveness, on the strength of its essentiality, the one withstands the other, asserts itself. Substantiveness is steadfastness, a determination to be *oneself*. Only the one who has a secure, solid foothold, who solidly *stands by him- or herself*, can also withstand the other. Essence is the self-same, which dwells in itself and thus delimits itself from the other. Essence or substance is characterized by a striving towards itself. The Greek notion of *hypostasis* means not only essence and foundation but also withstanding and steadfastness. And *stasis*, apart from standing, stand or standing place, also means revolt, discord and strife. According to its origins, essence is therefore anything but friendly. Only what is fully determined to be itself, what solidly stands by itself, what permanently *dwells* in itself – that is, what has the inwardness of essence – can enter into a conflict, into strife with the other. Without the determination to be oneself, which is the fundamental trait of essence, no strife is possible. Only the one who is able *fully to stay within him- or herself* even inside the other can have power. The figure of essence prefigures power. Because of this prefiguration, a culture, or thinking, that takes its cue from essence must necessarily develop a determination *to be oneself* that finds expression in the desire for power and possession.

In his *Monadology*, Leibniz rigorously draws out the ultimate consequences of the concept of substance.[4] The 'monad' represents this rigorous coming to a head and completion of essence. The monad *dwells* wholly in itself. There is no exchange with the outside. Thus, monads 'have no windows through which something can enter or leave'.[5] This total closure corresponds to the absolute inwardness of the windowless house. The monad's only impulse is its striving towards itself, self-affection, the *affect towards itself*, namely '*appetition*'. The inner life of the monad is guided simply by 'appetite', that is, 'perception'.[6] The monad is a 'mirror of the universe',[7] but it does not mirror the universe by abandoning itself to the things. Rather, the monad represents or expresses the universe. The monad is not passive but active or expressive, that is, ex-pressing. Leibniz's soul, as a 'living mirror', is a place of desiring.[8] The universe is simply an object of its 'appetition'. The monad perceives the universe because it has an appetite for it. It is this appetite alone that gives the world an independent *being*. *Existence* [Dasein] *is desire*. Without desire there is nothing. Thus, 'nothing is simpler and easier than something', than existence.[9] In order to exist, a striving, an effort, is required: 'Itaque dici potest Omne possibile Exisiturire.' ['Thus every possible can be said to strive to exist.'][10] The *verbum desiderativum* 'Existiturire' (wanting to be) signifies the 'conatus ad Existentiam' [striving towards existence]. What is present is characterized by exigency in its presencing; that is, it wants. It is the soul that *animates* existence to exigency. The *ground* of existence is exigency. The ground of being is wanting, which then, in particular in the modern age, takes the form of wanting *oneself*. Wanting, or even liking, *itself*, everything present must *accomplish* [erwirken] itself.

3

Heidegger, despite his efforts at leaving metaphysical thinking behind, and despite always seeking to get closer to Far Eastern thinking, remained a philosopher of essence, of the house and of dwelling. Although he retreated from quite a few of the intellectual patterns of metaphysics, the figure of 'essence' still dominated his thinking. Heidegger uses the term 'essence' almost excessively. The fundamental traits of essence, such as having a solid foothold, steadfastness, selfhood and duration, appear in various guises in his writings. Expressions like 'steadfastness', 'resoluteness of self' [Entschlossenheit zu sich], 'constancy of self' or 'self-constancy' dominate the vocabulary of his analysis of Dasein. He also connects strife and essence: 'In essential strife . . . the opponents raise each other into the self-assertion [Selbstbehauptung] of their essences.'[11]

As pointed out above, the dimension of strife (*stasis*) inheres in particular in the Greek idea of essence as *hypostasis*. Both the figure of strife and that of dialogue, frequently used by Heidegger, presuppose a bearer of essence, someone who presences [einen An-wesenden], that is, a person or individual who has a stand or standpoint, who is identical with him- or herself and stays the same. Those involved must properly be presencing [eigens an-wesend sein]. According to Heidegger, love consists in helping the other achieve his or her 'essence': 'Found the love! Probably the deepest interpretation of love is expressed in Augustine's word that says "amo volo ut sis", I love, that is, I want what I love to be what it is. Love is letting be in the deep sense in which it calls forth the essence.'[12]

Etymologically, the Chinese sign for being (*you*, 有) represents a hand that holds a piece of meat. *You* also means 'having' and 'possessing'. However, being as exigency, as appetition, does not dominate Chinese *thinking*. Quite the opposite – it is enthusiastically devoted to fasting. Daoist thinking makes use of a number of negations in order to

4

express that, *fundamentally*, existence is not an exigency, not an insistence, not a dwelling. The wise man 'wanders where there is nothing at all' (*you yu wu you*, 遊於無有).[13] Zhuangzi also speaks of wandering 'in simplicity' (*you yu dan*, 遊於淡).[14] Laozi also uses the 'not' (*wu*, 無) for negating 'essence' (*wu*, 物). The 'not a thing', the non-essence (*wu wu*, 無物) – we can say the ab-sencing [Ab-wesen] – evades all substantive determination.[15] It is consistent with this fact that non-essence is associated with wandering, with not-dwelling. The wise man wanders where there is 'no door and no house' (*wu men wu fang*, 無門無房).[16] He is compared to a quail that has no nest, that is, no home. He is 'a bird in flight that leaves no trail behind' (*niao xing er wu ji*, 鳥行而無跡).[17] The Daoist wandering is certainly not fully identical with the Buddhist 'non-dwelling' (*wu zhu*, 無住), but the negativity of absencing connects the two.[18] The Japanese Zen master Dōgen also teaches nowhere-dwelling: 'A Zen monk should be without fixed abode, like the clouds, and without fixed support, like water.'[19]

The good wanderer leaves no trace (*shan xing wu zhe ji*, 善行無轍跡). A trace points in a particular direction, and it points to an actor and his intention. Laozi's wanderer, by contrast, does not pursue any intention, and he does not go *to* any place. He walks in the 'directionless' (*wu fang*, 無方).[20] He completely fuses with the *way*, which does not lead *to* anywhere. *Traces* are created only in *being*. The fundamental *topos* of Far Eastern thinking is not being but the way (*dao*, 道). The way lacks the solidity of being and essence, which is what leads to the emergence of traces. There is no teleology to force it to follow a linear path. The *dao* is not a *poros*. Thus, it is freed of the possibility of possession and of the impossibility of the aporetic. This difference between *being* and *path*, between *dwelling* and *wandering*, between essence [Wesen] and absencing [Abwesen], is critical, and all of its

5

consequences must be spelled out. As opposed to being, the way does not permit any substantive closure. As it is endlessly processual, it does not allow anything to subsist, insist or persist. It therefore does not allow any fixed essences to come about. A *soul* insists. It consists of *traces*, so to speak. Absencing effaces it. In this effacing consists *emptiness*. Zhuangzi describes the wandering in absencing as follows: 'Already my will is vacant and blank. I go nowhere and don't know how far I've gotten. I go and come and don't know where to stop. I've already been there and back, and I don't know when the journey is done.'[21]

The wanderer *dwells nowhere*. The figure who recommends to *Tian Gen* – 'Heaven's Ground' – who is seeking his advice, to wander in non-being, is called 'Wu Ming' (無名, literally the 'nameless').[22] A name turns you into a *someone* in the strong sense. The wise man, by contrast, is nameless (*sheng ren wu ming*, 聖人無名).[23] He has 'no self' (*wu ji*, 無己, or *wu wo* 無我).[24] This topos of absence is to be found not only in Daoism but also in Confucius. In *Lunyu* it says: 'The master was without self.' The way the negation of the self is expressed in this case is unusual: the particle for negation, *wu* (毋), which always precedes a verb, here precedes the self and thereby negates it. Confucius *did not self*. He made nothing the content of his self.

From a certain perspective, in Chinese, being, that is, *you*, the hand that holds a piece of meat, is something quite prosaic. In order to exist, it seems to say, all that is needed is a piece of meat. Nurturing oneself is a prosaic act. As such, it has no exigency. It lacks the insistence of desiring. Zhuangzi even counts clothing oneself and eating among the *natural* virtues that human beings need to practice.[25] The belly (*fu*, 腹) does not desire. Desiring is based on the drawing of distinctions.[26] What desires is not the belly but the discriminating taste that strives for something specific (*wei*, 味). Laozi

6

demands: 'Empty the heart (*xu qi xin*, 虛其心), and fill the belly (*shi qi fu*, 實其腹). Weaken the will (*ruo qi zhi*, 弱其志), and strengthen the bones (*qiang qi gu*, 強其骨).'[27]

Merely to be sated and strong is certainly not a Daoist ideal. 'Belly' and 'bones' are here being used in figurative senses. They are organs of in-difference. Daoism does not pursue an ascetic ideal; having an empty heart does not categorically exclude having a full belly. With its determination and doggedness, asceticism is based to a large extent on desire. For this reason, Zhuangzi distances himself from ascetics and hermits. Bones are given another figurative sense in section 55 of the *Daodejing*, where the wise man is compared to a newborn child whose bones are 'supple' (*ruo*, 弱) and whose sinews are 'soft' (*rou*, 柔).[28] The weakness of the bones and softness of the sinews are opposed to the steadfastness of the essence that withstands and resists the other. Laozi might even have said: the wise man is without bones, like water.

In section 12 of the *Daodejing* the belly also figures as a non-desiring, non-distinguishing organ:

> The five colours turn a man's eyes blind;
> The five notes turn a man's ears deaf;
> The five tastes turn a man's palate dull;
>
> . . .
>
> For this reason,
> The ruling of the Sage is by the belly not by the eyes.[29]

This statement by Laozi is reminiscent of a provocative saying of the Zen master Linji: 'When you get hungry, eat your rice; / when you get sleepy, close your eyes. / Fools may laugh at me, / but wise men will know what I mean.'[30] And in Dōgen's *Shobogenzo* it says: 'In general, in the house of the Buddhist patriarchs, [drinking] tea and [eating] meals are everyday life itself.'[31]

7

Being – and on this point, at least, Laozi would agree with Leibniz – is more exhausting than non-being. Someone who exhausts himself, who struggles, remains in the realm of being. Non-being, the subtle and wondrous (*miao*, 妙), reveals itself only in 'non-struggling' (*bu qin*, 不勤). Emptiness, *xu* (虛), absencing, turns a someone into a no one. *No one is conspicuous by their absence.* Zhuangzi uses not only *xu* but also *kong* (空) to signify the emptying absencing:

> Bright Dazzlement [*Guang Yau*, literally 'glowing light'] asked Nonexistence, 'Sir, do you exist, or do you not exist?' Unable to obtain any answer, Bright Dazzlement stared intently at the other's face and form – all was vacuity and blankness [*kong*]. He stared all day but could see nothing, listened but could hear no sound, stretched out his hand but grasped nothing. 'Perfect!' exclaimed Bright Dazzlement. 'Who can reach such perfection?'[32]

Desire, appetition, is what makes you a *someone*. A *someone* in the strong sense has no access to wandering. A someone *dwells*. Only someone who empties himself and becomes a no one is able to wander. A wanderer is without an I, without a self, without a name. He forgets himself (*wang ji*, 忘己). He does not desire anything (*wu yu*, 無欲) and does not hold on to anything (*wu zhi*, 無執). He therefore does not leave a *trace*. Traces, the imprints left by holding on and desiring, form only in being. The wise man, however, does not touch being.

The Daoist teaching of *xu*, *absencing*, cannot be given a purely functional interpretation. It also elevates thinking above functional calculation. In section 15, Zhuangzi remarks: 'Emptiness, stillness, limpidity, silence, inaction – these are the level of Heaven and earth' (*tian dan ji mo, xu wu wu wei, ci tian di zhi ping*, 恬淡寂漠 虛無無為 此天地之平).[33] The term 'emptiness', *xu*, in the expression *xu wu* (虛無) bears no

8

functional meaning. When illustrating emptiness, the nothing and inaction, Laozi and Zhuangzi may use examples that permit a functional interpretation of emptiness or the nothing.[34] But the idea of effectiveness does not represent the essence of emptiness. François Jullien nevertheless interprets it almost exclusively from a functional perspective:

> This return to emptiness is stripped of all mysticism (given that nothing metaphysical is at stake). The Laozi recommends it in order to dissolve the blockages that threaten all reality as soon as no gaps remain in it and it becomes saturated. For if everything is filled, there is no room in which to operate. If emptiness is eliminated, the interplay that made it possible for the effect to be freely exercised is destroyed.[35]

At first sight, the story about the ghastly-looking cripple whose disability saves him from going to war, and who is instead amply supported by the state, seems to confirm the idea of efficacy. And there is certainly also a functional aspect to the anecdote about the cook who cuts up his meat so effortlessly because he follows the spaces in the joints of the cut rather than using blunt force, the meat falling apart with minimal effort. According to the functional interpretation, inaction increases the efficiency of an action. The story of the gnarled tree that grows to a ripe old age because of its uselessness also admits of a utilitarian interpretation: the absence of usefulness can be useful. However, the fact that so many cripples and so many useless things populate Zhuangzi's stories leads functionality itself into emptiness. The role of Zhuangzi's one-legged, hump-backed, misshaped, toeless and footless characters is to demonstrate that all worries about usefulness and efficiency are superfluous. Laozi and Zhuangzi vehemently oppose all desire to bring about effects. At first sight, sections 68 and 69 of Laozi also seem to talk about the efficacy

9

of inaction. In section 68, for instance, he says: 'Those good at overcoming enemies do not fight them.'[36] François Jullien interprets this remark purely in terms of strategy. Instead of deploying a large amount of energy in order to bring about an effect, the wise simply let it happen. They can 'effortlessly use the energy of others'.[37] Jullien also gives section 69 a purely functional interpretation:

> The Laozi then applies this principle to military strategy. A good leader in war is not 'bellicose,' that is – as the commentator Wang Bi understands it – he does not try to take the initiative and be aggressive. In other words, 'he who is capable of defeating the enemy does not engage in battle with him.'[38]

A good military leader simply ensures that the enemy is unable to find a line of attack. Pressure is exerted on the opponent, but this pressure 'does not manifest itself at all in a localized fashion'.[39] A wise strategist sees to it that the opponent is not offered anything tangible:

> The Laozi explains the situation using a set of paradoxical expressions . . . 'marching on an expedition without there being any expedition' or 'rolling up one's sleeves without there being any arms there' or 'pressing forward to battle without there being any enemy' or 'holding absent weapons firmly in hand' (section 69).[40]

Interestingly, Jullien's interpretation does not mention the last, decisive passage of section 69: '*the one that grieves will win*' (*ai zhe sheng*, 哀者勝). Laozi's conclusion here is very surprising. It almost compels us to interpret this paragraph in a completely different way. For 'grief' (*ai*, 哀) is not a part of any military strategy, including that of Sun Tzu, who believes in the efficacy of detours, of indirect means. The victory the passage talks about is not a real victory that would be owed to a particular military strategy. Rather, it is a victory that stands above the *distinction* between 'victory' and 'defeat'. Laozi uses the sign for 'grief', 'ai', exactly two times. The other occurrence is in section 31. Interestingly, this paragraph also treats of war. Jullien, however, does not mention this paragraph. The reason he doesn't is simple: in it, Laozi condemns all use of weapons, and not because the wise military leader must be able to defeat his enemies without weapons, but simply out of benevolence. On 'festive occasions', the place of honour is on the left, but at 'funerals' it is the right. Those who have been victorious in battle must stand on the right side. The victor has to take his place according to the customary grieving ritual (*ai li*, 哀禮). He has to 'lament' (*bei*, 悲), 'grieve' (*ai*, 哀) and 'cry' (*qi*, 泣).[41]

Both Daoist and Buddhist thought distrust any substantive closedness that subsists, closes itself off and perseveres. With regard to absencing, understood in an active sense, the Buddhist teaching of *kong* (空) is certainly related to Daoist emptiness, *xu* (虛). Both bring about an *absencing* heart, empty the self into a non-self, into a no one, into someone 'nameless'. This *xu* of the *heart* resists functional interpretation. With *xu*, Zhuangzi expresses primarily non-exigent being, absencing. Zhuangzi's empty mirror differs radically from Leibniz's mirror with a *soul*, because it does not possess any exigential inwardness, any 'appetition'. It does not desire anything, does not hold on to anything. It is empty and absencing. In this way, it lets the things it mirrors come and go. It goes *along*, not *ahead*. Thus, it does not *lose its way*, does not violate anything:

> The Perfect Man uses his mind like a mirror – going after nothing, welcoming nothing, responding but not storing . . .

He is not a master (*zhu*, 主) of insights. He takes note of the minutest things, and yet is inexhaustible and dwells beyond the I. Down to the last thing, he receives what Heaven provides, and yet he holds it as if he held nothing.[42]

In section 13, Zhuangzi also uses the metaphor of the mirror:

The ten thousand things are insufficient to distract his mind – that is the reason he is still. Water that is still gives back a clear image of beard and eyebrows . . . And if water in stillness possesses such clarity, how much more must pure spirit. The sage's mind in stillness is the mirror of Heaven and earth.[43]

Zen Buddhism also likes to draw on the rhetorical figure of the mirror in order to illustrate the not-holding-on of the 'empty heart' (*wu xin*, 無心):

The mirror . . . remains as it is: empty in itself . . . This is Hui-neng's mirror; this is also Hsua-feng's mirror . . . But what a mirroring! And what is it that is mirrored in it? There is the earth and sky; there are mountains rising and waters streaming; there is grass greening and trees growing. And in springtime, hundreds of flowers blossom . . . Is there an intention behind all this, a meaning that one could conceive? Isn't all this simply there? . . . But only a clear mirror that is empty in itself, only someone who has realized the nullity of the world and of himself, also sees the eternal beauty in it.[44]

The empty mirror is based on the absence of the desiring self, on a heart that is *fasting*. By contrast, Fichte, the philosopher of the I and of action, scorns the empty heart:

The system of freedom satisfies my heart; the opposite system destroys and annihilates it. To stand, cold and unmoved, amid the current of events, a passive mirror of fugitive and passing phenomena, this existence is insupportable to me; I scorn and detest it. I will love: I will lose myself in sympathy; I will know the joy and the grief of life. I myself am the highest object of this sympathy.[45]

Originally, the German word 'Sinn' (sense; Middle High German: *sin*) also meant 'walk', 'journey' and 'path'. But it is associated with a particular direction, a particular destination. The expression 'Uhrzeigersinn' (clockwise), for instance, points towards the direction in which the clock's hand moves. The French 'sens' still carries the meaning of 'direction' or 'side'. Wandering in non-being, by contrast, is 'without direction', hence 'sense-less' [sinn-los] or 'empty of sense' [sinn-entleert]. It is just this freedom from meaning, from a direction, a destination, this specific kind of emptiness of sense that makes a higher freedom, even *being*, possible in the first place. Being in harmony with the directionless and unlimited totality before any distinction is posited brings 'heavenly joy' (*tian le*, 天樂), 'supreme happiness' (*zhi le*, 至樂).[46] Fortune (*fu*, 福), by contrast, rests on a distinction or preference, on a partial perception. Someone who wants to be lucky thereby exposes himself to misfortune. The aim is not to be the 'bearer of good fortune or the initiator of bad fortune' (*bu wei fu xian, bu wei huo shi*, 不為福先, 不為禍始).[47] The absence of *sense* leads not to nihilism but to a heavenly joy about *being*, a being without direction or trace.

Zhuangzi's teaching of supreme happiness is the exact opposite of Kant's theory of happiness. In his *Anthropology from a Pragmatic Point of View*, Kant remarks that 'filling our time by means of methodical, progressive occupations that lead to an important and intended end . . . is the only sure means of becoming happy with one's life and, at the same time satiated with life'.[48] He compares life to a journey

13

on which 'the *abundance* of objects seen . . . produces in our memory the . . . conclusion that a vast amount of space has been covered and, consequently, that a longer period of time necessary for this purpose has also passed', while '*emptiness*', that is, the absence of objects to be perceived, in hindsight produces the feeling that a shorter period of time has passed.[49] Thus, subjectively, emptiness shortens life. In order to become satiated with life, in order to enjoy it, no period of one's life should be 'empty'. Only a life that is filled with goal-directed actions is a happy and satisfying life. Sense is goal. Being is doing. Laozi and Zhuangzi, on the contrary, are convinced that a completely different project of Dasein, a completely different world, is possible. They juxtapose a directionless, a-teleological wandering with that linear, teleological, even vectorial design for life. Their project for Dasein does without sense and goal, without teleology and narration, without transcendence and God. In it, the absence of sense and goal is not a deprivation; rather, it means greater freedom, a *more coming from less*. Only through dropping the walking-*towards* does walking actually become possible. The world whose natural course [Gang] human beings need to follow has no *narrative* structure. It is therefore also resistant to the crisis of meaning [Sinnkrise], which is always a narrative crisis. The world tells neither 'grand' nor 'small' narratives. It is not a *myth* but *nature* in a particular sense. For that very reason, it is *grand*. All narrations are *small* in comparison, because every narration is based on a *distinction* that excludes one thing in favour of another. Narration that founds meaning is the result of a massive operation of selection and exclusion, even of a *shrinking* of the world. The world is pushed on to a narrow narrative path and reduced. Zhuangzi therefore teaches that one should associate oneself with the *whole* world, even to be *as large* as the world, to elevate oneself to a wide world, instead of clinging on to a small narrative, a small distinction. For that reason, his wondrous stories are often populated by gigantic figures. In fact, the very first anecdote he presents tells of a giant fish named Kun and a giant bird by the name of Peng:

In the bald and barren north, there is a dark sea, the Lake of Heaven. In it is a fish that is several thousand *li* across, and no one knows how long . . . There is also a bird there . . . with a back like Mount Tai and wings like clouds filling the sky. He beats the whirlwind, leaps into the air, and rises up ninety thousand *li*, cutting through the clouds and mist, shouldering the blue sky, and then he turns his eyes south and prepares to journey to the southern darkness.[50]

Kun and Peng are too gigantic to fit small things; they elevate themselves above all, excluding selection and distinction. They do not care about small things; they are simply *too big* for that. Zhuangzi purposefully uses excessive dimensions and exaggeration in order to suspend distinctions, to achieve a *de-differentiation* and *un-bounding*.

Someone who is not tied to a particular thing or place, who wanders and dwells nowhere, is beyond the possibility of loss. Someone who does not possess anything specific cannot lose anything:

You hide your boat in the ravine and your fish net in the swamp and tell yourself that they will be safe. But in the middle of the night, a strong man shoulders them and carries them off, and in your stupidity, you don't know why it happened. You think you do right to hide little things in big ones, and yet they get away from you. But if you were to hide the world in the world, so that nothing could get away, this would be the final reality of the constancy of things.[51]

15

In this passage, Zhuangzi talks about a special relationship to the world. The demand is to un-bound and de-differentiate the being-*in*-the-world into a being-*world*. As long as it is *smaller* than the world, as long as it *draws distinctions* within the world, the human being, or, to speak with Heidegger, Dasein, will be affected by *care*. To free *itself of care*, it must be *the* entire *world*, must de-differentiate *itself* into the world, instead of clinging on to a particular element of the world or distinction. Being-*in*-the-world is being afflicted by care. Being-*world*, by contrast, is free of care.

Of course, postmodern thinkers also oppose ideas of substance and identity. Derrida's 'différance' and Deleuze's 'rhizome' radically question substantive closure and closedness, exposing them as imagined constructions. The negativity of these thinkers brings them close to absencing and emptiness, but the idea, typical of Far Eastern thinking, of a *world-like totality*, of the *weight of the world*, is alien to them, as it is to all postmodern thought. In Far Eastern thinking, emptiness or absencing ultimately has a collecting or gathering effect, whereas 'différance' or 'rhizome' cause an intense form of dispersal. They disperse identity, push diversity. Their care is not a care for the totality, for its harmony and accord. The Far Eastern thinking of emptiness leaves deconstruction behind in order to achieve a special kind of reconstruction.

Far Eastern thinking turns completely towards immanence. The *dao*, for instance, does not represent some monumental, supernatural or super-sensual entity that can only be talked about in negative terms, as in negative theology; it does not flee from immanence in favour of something transcendent. The *dao* merges fully with worldly immanence, with the 'this-is-how-it-is' of things, with the here and now. In the Far Eastern imagination, there is nothing outside the immanence of the world. It is not because it is *too high* that the *dao* escapes definition or direct naming; it is because it *flows*, because it *meanders*, so to speak. It signifies the permanent transformation of things, the procedural nature of the world. The wanderer leaves no trace behind because he remains in step with the wandering of things. The *dao* is also not a 'lord' over things, not a subject (*zhu*, 主).[52] It does not retreat into secrecy. It is characterized by immanence and the natural evidence of the 'this-is-how-it-is'. Laozi therefore emphasizes that his words are 'most easy to understand' (*shen yi zhi*, 甚易知) and 'most easy to practice' (*shen yi xing*, 甚易行).[53]

The fact that the wanderer leaves no trace behind also has a temporal significance. He does not insist or persist. Rather, he exists in the actual. As he 'moves in the directionless', he does not walk along a linear, historical time that stretches into past and future.[54] The care that Heidegger gives the status of being the fundamental trait of human existence is tied to this stretched-out, historical time. The wanderer does not exist historically. Thus, he is 'without care' (*bu si lu*, 不思慮) and 'does not ponder or scheme, does not plot for the future' (*bu yu mou*, 不豫謀).[55] The sage exists neither looking backwards nor forwards. Rather, he lives in the present. He *dwells* in *every* present, but the present does not have the sharpness or determinacy of the momentous. The moment is tied to the vigour and determination of doing. The sage exists situationally. This situationality, however, differs from Heidegger's 'situation', which is based on the determination inherent in actions and on the moment. In Heidegger's situation, Dasein resolutely takes hold of *itself*. This situation is the supreme moment of *presence*. The wanderer dwells in every instant, but he does not *linger*, because in lingering the focus is too much on objects. The wanderer leaves no trace because he dwells without *lingering*.

Zhuangzi's famous story of the 'butterfly dream' is therefore suffused with an atmosphere of absence. He imagines a form of Dasein that lacks all solidity, definiteness, all exigential determinacy and finality. The story illustrates a Dasein without 'care':

Once Zhuang Zhou dreamed he was a butterfly, a butterfly flitting and fluttering around, happy with himself and doing as he pleased. He didn't know he was Zhuang Zhou. Suddenly he woke up, and there he was, solid and unmistakable Zhuang Zhou. But he didn't know if he were Zhuang Zhou who had dreamed he was a butterfly or a butterfly dreaming he was Zhuang Zhou.[56]

Oblivious to his self, Zhuangzi hovers between himself and all else. He abandons himself to a specific kind of indifference. This hovering is opposed to that steadfastness that represents the fundamental trait of essencing. Steadfastness makes it possible for someone to dwell within himself, cling on to himself, and thus to withstand the other and distinguish himself from the other. Absencing, by contrast, spreads across Dasein something dream-like and hovering, because it makes it impossible to give an unambiguous, final, that is, substantial, contour to things. Zhuangzi would respond to the concept of the individual, that is, the indivisible, by saying that he is infinitely dividable, infinitely transformable. Zhuangzi's dream is a dream without soul, a dream that is not made up of *traces*. *No one dreams.* His dream is an *absolute dream*, because the world is *itself* a dream. The dream is therefore beyond the reach of theories of the soul, psychology or psychoanalysis. The dreaming subject is neither 'ego' nor 'id'. The world itself dreams. The world is a dream. Absencing maintains everything in a dream-like hovering.

It is only with the influence of Buddhism that Chinese culture begins to develop a deep sensitivity for the transience and fleetingness of being. Buddhism is ultimately a religion of

18

absence, of fading out and blowing away, a religion of 'dwelling nowhere'.[57] The Chinese culture and art of blandness would be inconceivable without Buddhism.[58] The Chinese aesthetics of blandness is animated in particular by a sensitivity for the painful charm of transience. The poets of blandness mainly sing of the tender shine of the transient. The Japanese wandering monk Bashō begins the diary of his travels with words from the Chinese poet Li Bo:[59]

> Heaven and earth – the whole cosmos – is just a guest house;
>   it hosts all beings together.
> Sun and moon are also just guests in it, passing guests in
>   eternal times.
> Life in this fleeting world is like a dream.
> Who knows how many more times we are going to laugh?
> Our ancestors therefore lit candles in praise of the night.[60]

Absencing does not allow for the taking of sides. Any preference for one side would disadvantage the other. Any inclination implies disinclination. Instead, the aim is to 'embrace the ten thousand things universally' (*jian huai wan wu*, 兼懷萬物).[61] Love and friendship presuppose making distinctions and taking sides. They rest on *appetition*. For these reasons, the sage 'has no love for men' (*bu wei ai ren*, 不為愛人) and has 'no more likes' (*qin*, 親), that is, does not cultivate friendships.[62] Love is something insisting, and friendship creates ties. The sage is not, however, completely detached. Disinterestedness presupposes a coherent subject who could have interests but for whom the world has become unimportant. Absencing does not empty love and friendship and make them irrelevant. It turns them into bound-less *friendliness*. This friendliness consists in embracing everything with complete impartiality.

Kafka's story 'The Cares of a Family Man' reads like one of Zhuangzi's wondrous tales. The 'creature called Odradek' is really an absencing.[63] This strange creature, whose shape is that of a 'flat star-shaped spool for thread', is so multiform that it evades any unambiguous definition of an essence. The name already defies unambiguity: 'Some say the word Odradek is of Slavonian origin, and try to account for it on that basis. Others again believe it to be of German origin, only influenced by Slavonic. The uncertainty of both interpretations allows one to assume with justice that neither is accurate, especially as neither of them provides an intelligent meaning of the word.' In addition, Odradek is a motley combination of parts that appear to differ in their essence. Leibniz's monads, as 'simple substances' (*substance simple*), by contrast, have 'no parts' (*sans parties*).[64] Like Plato's beauty, a monad is 'always one in form' (*monoeides*).[65] Odradek is an absencing, even a non-essence [Ab-, ja ein Un-Wesen], in the sense that he is composed of the most heterogeneous parts. His appearance is hybrid, as if he wanted to mock the unambiguity of essences:

> At first glance it looks like a flat star-shaped spool for thread, and indeed it does seem to have thread wound upon it; to be sure, they are only old, broken-off bits of thread, knotted and tangled together, of the most varied sorts and colors. But it is not only a spool, for a small wooden crossbar sticks out of the middle of the star, and another small rod is joined to that at a right angle. By means of this latter rod on one side and one of the points of the star on the other, the whole thing can stand upright as if on two legs.

His 'diminutive' figure also evokes the impression of an absencing. Because of his diminutiveness, it is impossible to get hold of him. He is 'extraordinarily nimble and can never be laid hold of'. He lacks any of the solidity of an essence. His extreme nimbleness is opposed to the tenacity of essences.

He also seems to be absent because he often retreats into muteness. Occasionally, he laughs, but his laughter sounds oddly bodyless and empty. This strengthens the impression of absencing: 'it is only the kind of laughter that has no lungs behind it. It sounds rather like the rustling of fallen leaves.'

Odradek could easily join the circle of hump-backed, one-legged, footless or toeless figures and other strange, useless creatures that populate Zhuangzi's anecdotes. Zhuangzi's gnarled tree reaches a ripe old age because it is useless. Similarly, Odradek appears to transcend usefulness: 'Can he possibly die? Anything that dies has had some kind of aim in life, some kind of activity, which has worn out; but that does not apply to Odradek.' Odradek is also ab-sencing because he never lingers in one place. He lives nowhere. He is a counter-figure to the inwardness of the home. Asked 'And where do you live?' his habitual answer is 'No fixed abode'. Even when he is inside a house, he can usually be found only in places that are *devoid of inwardness*, such as 'the garret, the stairway, the lobbies, the entrance hall'. He is thus not fully at home, not fully with himself. He seems to avoid *closed* rooms. Often he is simply *absent*: 'Often for months on end he is not to be seen.' This absence, this non-dwelling, unsettles the 'family man' who takes care of the house. The 'care of the family man' is about the absence of Odradek. We may even say that the family man is *care itself*. Odradek, who is free of any cares, is his opposite. It is clear, however, that Odradek is ultimately not one of Zhuangzi's creations, because despite his long absences, which trouble the family man so much, Odradek, as Kafka writes, 'always comes faithfully back to our house again'.

Closed and Open – Spaces of Absencing

In the Far East, far more than in the West, the way things flow into each other is openly visible. In the narrow shopping lanes, it is not always clear where one shop ends and another one begins. Often, they overlap. In a Korean market, pots and pans appear next to dried squid. Lipstick and peanuts lie next to each other. Skirts hang above rice cakes. The tangle of electricity poles, wiring and colourful advertisements one often finds in Japanese cities does not allow for an unambiguous separation of spaces. The old wooden houses in Japanese backstreets (*roji*) appear to nestle in one another. It is not easy to see where one house ends and the next one begins. This spatiality of in-difference is reminiscent of a Zen saying: 'When snow covers the white flowers, it's hard to distinguish the outlines.'[1] It is difficult to distinguish between the white of the flowers and the white of the snow. Essence is difference. Thus, essences block transitions. Absencing is in-difference. It liquefies and un-bounds. The river landscape in snow (illustration 1) is a *landscape of absencing*. Nothing

22

Illustration 1: Hovering landscape

imposes itself. Nothing demarcates itself from other things. Everything appears to retreat into an in difference.

One rarely finds flowing transitions in the West. The presence of strong boundaries and delimitations creates a feeling of narrowness. By contrast, despite the crowds of people and the density of the housing, Far Eastern cities appear as places of emptiness and absencing.

An absencing gaze has an emptying effect. Flowing transitions create places of absencing and emptiness. Essences have a closing and excluding effect. Absencing, by contrast, makes space more permeable. Thus, it widens space. A space makes space for another space. A space opens itself up for another space. There is no final closure.[2] The space of emptiness, the de-internalized space, consists of transitions and in-between spaces. Amid the hustle and bustle of Far Eastern cities there is thus a soothing emptiness, even a *bustling emptiness*.

In-difference also fosters an intense side-by-side of what is different. It creates an optimal degree of cohesion with a

23

minimal amount of organic, organized connection. Synthetic composition gives way to a syndetic continuum of closeness in which things do not come together as a unity. They are not members in the sense of *elements* of an organic totality. This gives them a *friendly* appearance. Membership does not create a *friendly neighbourhood*. In the syndetic continuum, there is no need for a dialogue to mediate between things or reconcile them. They do not have much to *do* with each other. Rather, they empty themselves into an in-different closeness.

Western culture is determined to pursue closedness and closure. Interestingly, this determination is reflected not only in the metaphysical figure of 'substance' but also in Western architecture. For example, Leibniz's monadic, windowless soul finds a counterpart in that fundamental form of the Romantic architecture that Hegel calls 'the fully enclosed house'.[3] Beauty finds its perfection in classical art. But Romantic art, according to Hegel, expresses something superior to classical art, because Romantic art is about inwardness. As opposed to classical art, which simply radiates outwards, Romantic art radiates an inner brilliance, a brilliance of inwardness. This Romantic inwardness unfolds in a 'fully enclosed house', a 'totally enclosed' space in which the outside is blotted out.[4] According to Hegel, the Christian religion is a religion of inwardness, and therefore finds its external correlate in the *fully closed* place of worship

> Just as the Christian spirit concentrates itself in the inner life, so the building becomes shut in on every side for the assembly of the Christian congregation and the collection of its thoughts. The spatial enclosure corresponds to the concentration of mind within, and results from it.[5]

The portal of the place of worship initiates the process of internalization by narrowing towards the inside. This 'nar-

24

Illustration 2: City without thresholds

rowing due to perspective' announces 'that the exterior has to shrink, contract, and disappear'.[6] The colonnades, originally half inside, half outside, are moved inside the building, where they form an internalized, even *internal*, outside. Natural light is not allowed to shine directly into the inner space because it would disturb the inner concentration. It is therefore 'excluded or it only glimmers dimly through windows of the stained glass necessary for complete separation from the outside world'.[7] The external natural light is blocked. Everything external as such has to be shed in favour of inwardness. The external distracts, and thereby impairs inner concentration. The place of worship has to be filled with a purely inner light, a divine light. The windows are actually not openings;

rather, they serve the purpose of 'complete separation from the outside world'. Hegel emphasizes that they are 'only half-transparent'.[8] Their dimming of the light lends inwardness to the space. The windowpanes are also not *empty*. They are painted, that is, *saturated* with meaning. The glass paintings, which often depict Christ's Passion, suffuse the light with *meaningfulness*, thereby further intensifying the inwardness, the fullness of the inner space.

A Buddhist temple is not a completely open house. A Greek temple, by contrast, is fully open; its open passageways and halls represent a *passing-through* of the divine, of divine wind.[9] This openness, however, is a *being-exposed*. A Buddhist temple is neither fully closed nor fully open. Its spatiality effects neither an inwardness nor a being-exposed. Rather, its spaces are *empty*. The space of emptiness maintains the in-difference between open and closed, within and without. The Buddhist temple hall has barely any walls. On its sides, it is surrounded by numerous doors of translucent rice paper. The function of the paper is not to make sure that light 'only glimmers dimly' inside so that, as in the case of a cathedral, the inwardness of the space is not affected. As opposed to stained-glass windows, the paper does not serve the purpose of 'complete separation from the outside world'. Because of the low roof, only faint light – like a *re-flected brilliance* [Ab-glanz] – reaches the doors anyhow. This light is already characterized by an *absence*. Like a sponge, the matt-white paper softly soaks up the already dimmed light and brings it to a total standstill, so to speak. The result is a *standing light*, a light that is therefore not *blinding*. The low roof also removes all verticality from the light. The light does not *fall down from above* as it does in a cathedral. And the paper takes away all of the light's movement and directionality. There thus emerges a standing pool of still light. This special light is, to use a Daoist expression, 'without direction'. It does not illumine or shine on anything.

26

Illustration 3: Where does the inside begin?

The standing light, which has become fully indeterminate, in-different, does not emphasize the presence of things: it submerges them in an absence. White is, after all, the colour of in-difference par excellence. The white, empty paper is opposed to the colourful, stained-glass windows. Colours intensify presence. The matt-white light has the same effect as that snow along the riverbank that creates a landscape of absence, of in-difference. This light of in-difference, this in-between light, enwraps everything in an atmosphere of emptiness and absence.

The light that comes to stand still at the opaque, white sliding paper doors also distinguishes the openness of Far Eastern architecture from the unimpeded *transparency* of modern glass architecture, a transparency that gives this form of architecture an appearance of unfriendliness. Light, in this case, aggressively falls into the inside. This architecture is not indebted to Far Eastern openness but to Plato's and Plotinus' metaphysics of light. Plato's dark cave and the blinding light of the sun outside belong to the same topography of being. Far Eastern spatiality, by contrast, elevates itself above the dichotomy of open and closed, inside and outside, light and shadow, and creates an in-difference, an in-between. The smooth, glittering surface of glass and metal also emphasizes presence, and it is therefore opposed to the friendly restraint and reticence of the matt-white rice paper. Rice paper possesses a materiality of emptiness and absence. Its surface does not shine, and it is as soft as silk. When folded, it hardly makes a noise, as if it were stillness itself, condensed in matt white.

The verticality of the light that enters a cathedral is strengthened by the arrangement of the windows. The upper windows of the nave and the choir are so massive that they cannot be taken in in one glance, so the gaze is pulled upwards. This vertical movement of the gaze generates a 'restlessness of rising up'.[10] Other architectural elements, such as pillars and pointed arches, also generate a feeling of upward striving or rising:

> The pillars become thin and slender and rise so high that the eye cannot take in the whole shape at a single glance but is driven to travel over it and to rise until it begins to find rest in the gently inclined vaulting of the arches that meet, just as the worshipping heart, restless and troubled at first, rises above the territory of finitude and finds rest in God alone.[11]

Hegel juxtaposes these spatial effects of Gothic architecture to those of Greek temples, where horizontality, weight and bearing are typical: 'Thus, while the buildings of classical architecture in the main lie on the ground horizontally, the opposite romantic character of Christian churches consists in their growing out of the ground and rising to the sky.'[12]

28

Neither upward striving nor horizontality or weight bring about the spatial effect of a Buddhist temple. One cannot read any striving against gravity, against the 'ground of finitude', into its architectural elements. And the lightness of the materials used is such that any impression of weight or persistence is avoided. Indeed, emptiness has *no weight*. And no divine presence *weighs* on the space. Despite all their differences, the Greek temple and the cathedral are both *towering*. A Buddhist temple never appears to tower, as a Greek temple does. The spatial characteristics of the Buddhist temple are not those of standing or steadfastness, the fundamental traits of essences. Buddhist temples in the Far East are also often to be found in forest clearings, surrounded and protected by mountainsides. And they lie *aside*, whereas cathedrals and Greek temples mark and occupy the *centre*. In this sense, too, Buddhist temples are absent.

Straight lines cannot express inwardness. Inwardness is a form of return to oneself. It is *bent*. Thus, it prefers to dwell in curves and turns. Square spaces are also unsuitable places for Romantic, infinite inwardness:

> The movement of the spirit with the distinctions it makes and its conciliation of them in the course of its elevation from the terrestrial to the infinite, to the loftier beyond, would not be expressed architecturally in this empty uniformity of a quadrilateral.[13]

In contrast to Christian churches, in Buddhist temples lines and square forms are prevalent, and these prevent the formation of inwardness. Japanese Zen monasteries and tea houses often have asymmetrical features. Asymmetry (*fukinsei*) is an aesthetic principle of Zen Buddhism.[14] It introduces a rupture into space. Symmetrical regularity stresses presence. Asymmetry *breaks* up presence into absencing.

According to Hegel's philosophical physiognomy, the eyes should be surrounded by the elevated bones so that 'the strengthened shadow in the orbits gives us of itself a feeling of depth and undistracted inner life'.[15] The 'sharply cut outline of the orbits' announces the deep inwardness of the soul.[16] Thus, 'the eye, that is to say, should not protrude or, as it were, project itself into the external world'.[17] Eastern eyes, of course, are flat. Hegel would explain this in terms of a lack of inwardness, that is, an infantile spirit that has not yet awoken to subjective inwardness and therefore remains embedded in nature. Hegel also points out the 'sightlessness' of Greek sculptures of the gods.[18] Their eyes do not yet have that fire of the inner soul; Greek sculptures do 'not express the movement and activity of the spirit which has retired into itself out of its corporeal reality and made its way to inner self-awareness'.[19] Far Eastern thinking cannot be brought into the context of this distinction between inner and outer, inwardness and outwardness. It dwells in a zone of in-difference, an *in-between* that is both *de-internalized and de-externalized. Emptiness is neither inside nor outside.* Hegel's philosophy of inwardness does not capture the *absencing* gaze that is neither absorbed in the inner nor immersed in and distracted by the outer. That gaze is simply *empty*.

In his essay on surrealism, Walter Benjamin talks about the Buddhist monks who vowed never to stay in closed rooms. How uncanny these Tibetan monks must have appeared to Benjamin, who grew up with the bourgeois inwardness of the nineteenth century:

> In Moscow I lived in a hotel in which almost all the rooms were occupied by Tibetan lamas who had come to Moscow for a congress of Buddhist churches. I was struck by the number of doors in the corridors that were always left ajar. What had at first seemed accidental began to be disturbing.

Illustration 4: A room without inwardness

I found out that in these rooms lived members of a sect who had sworn never to occupy closed rooms.[20]

Benjamin would probably find it easier to have sympathy for Marcel Proust, who, having decided to dedicate his life to writing, sealed off his room with three layers of curtains. The walls were plastered with corkboard. No daylight or street noise was to enter his room. Writing as the *remembrance* [Erinnerung] and *internalization* of the world takes place in a hermetically sealed room of absolute inwardness; it could even be called a cathedral of inwardness.

31

Light and Shadow – The Aesthetics of Absencing

A kabuki actor explains that he particularly loves peonies because they lose their petals in an instant. It is not only the fully blooming peony, in all its splendour, that is beautiful; what is most beautiful of all is the painful charm of its transience. The actor apparently admires the fact that peonies cast off their petals without any hesitation, so to speak, that they are content to disappear, instead of slowly withering away, even though this is *against nature* – because *nature* is *appetitus*, the *conatus ad Existentiam*, holding on to existence. The kabuki actor maybe sees a kind of *sartori*, Zen Buddhist illumination, in the flower's releasement – *Gelassenheit* – when passing away, in its in-difference towards life and death. Its unnatural in-difference appears to him as a reflection of the spirit that has thrown off the *soul* and its *natural* desire altogether.

Kant, in his *Critique of Judgment*, calls it 'worthy of note' that, if we 'secretly played a trick' on a 'lover of the beautiful, sticking in the ground artificial flowers', and if 'he then discovered the deceit', then 'the direct interest he previously took in these things would promptly vanish'. This lover of the beautiful may possibly find the shape of the artificial flowers beautiful. But he does not like their Dasein, their existence, because they are not *creations* of nature: 'the thought that the beauty in question was produced by nature must accompany the intuition and the reflection, and the direct interest we take in that beauty is based on that thought alone'.[1] The flowers' artificiality deprives them of their *teleological*, even *theological*, significance. If nature were to bring forth a flower that never withered, its imperishable splendour would most likely delight Kant's lover of the beautiful and make him happy. Its imperishable, indestructible, everlasting existence would not take anything away from the feeling of beauty. Quite the contrary, it would intensify it. For Plato, too, divine beauty is an everlasting being that neither emerges nor vanishes, neither increases nor decreases.

Yoshida Kenkō, in his *The Miscellany of a Japanese Priest*, writes:

Is it only when the flowers are in full bloom and when the moon is shining in spotless perfection that we ought to gaze at them? . . . The twigs which bear no blossoms as yet and a garden strewn with withered petals are equally to be admired . . . Incomparably more touching than gazing at a spotless full moon in other far distant lands is it to wait and watch till when near daybreak it appears pale and solitary above the branches of the cedars in the wild mountains, to note the shadows between the trees, and how all grows dim beneath the clustering clouds as gentle rain begins to fall.[2]

In the sensibility of the Far East, neither the permanence [Ständigkeit] of *being* nor the stability [Beständigkeit] of *essences* is part of the beautiful. Things that persist, subsist or insist are neither beautiful nor noble. Beautiful is not

33

Illustration 5: Bright without light

what stands out or exceeds but what exercises self-restraint or retreats, not what is solid but what hovers. Beautiful are things that carry the traces of nothingness, even of their own end in themselves, things that do not resemble their *selves*. What is beautiful is not the duration of a *condition* [Zustandes] but the fleetingness of a *transition*. What is beautiful is not full presence but a 'there' that is coated with an absence, that is made *lighter* or *less* by *emptiness*. What is beautiful is not what is clear or transparent but what is not clearly delineated, not clearly distinguished (which must, however, not be confused with what is diffuse). Diffusion, like indeterminacy, is a condition that can be rectified by the adding of definitions and the making of distinctions. It awaits precision. The condition of in-difference, by contrast, is already *evident in itself*. It is self-sufficient, has its own *determinacy*. In-difference does not mean that there is a lack of differences or distinctions. In-difference does not lack anything.

The Japanese notion of 'wabi-sabi' refers to a particular style that combines the unfinished, the imperfect, the transient, the fragile and the unassuming, and it expresses a genuinely Buddhist feeling of beauty. For instance, tea vessels in the wabi style must not look perfect and immaculate. Rather, they need to be broken in themselves. Irregularities and asym-

34

metry are therefore intentionally built into them. A famous example of something that expresses wabi principles, from the master of tea ceremonies Shukō, is a thoroughbred horse that is tied up in front of a small hut with a straw roof. Wabi is, for instance, a *single* plum tree twig flowering in deep snow. Wabi is juxtaposed with the magnificent, perfect, grand, opulent, expansive and unchanging. What is beautiful is a silver bowl that has lost its sheen and begun to darken. What is beautiful is not what is bright, translucent or crystalline but what is matt, cloud-like, clouded over, what is semi-translucent or shadowy. In his book *In Praise of Shadows*, Tanizaki Junichiro writes: 'The Chinese also love jade. That strange lump of stone with its faintly muddy light, like the crystallized air of the centuries, melting dimly, dully back, deeper and deeper – are not we Orientals the only ones who know its charms?'[3]

Satori (illumination) actually has nothing to do with shining or light. This is another point on which Eastern spirituality differs from occidental mysticism, with its metaphysics of light. Light multiplies presence. Buddhism, however, is a religion of absence. Thus, nirvana, the Sanskrit expression for illumination, originally meant 'fading out'. To restrain oneself, to be absent, is the Buddhist ideal. The Far East has a very cautious attitude towards light. It does not know of that heroic light that seeks to reduce the darkness. Rather, light and darkness cling to each other. This in-difference of light and darkness is also typical of Zen Buddhist ink drawings. Their backgrounds are an evenly lit matt white. The figures seem to be there only to bring out the white of the paper. Earth and sky, mountains and water, flow into each other, creating a hovering landscape of emptiness. The light in the pictures is also *directionless*. It suffuses the landscape in a mood of absence. Earth and sky have the same brightness. It is not clear where the earth ends and the sky begins, where the light ends and darkness begins.

Illustration 6: The blinding light of the angel

East Asia's light of absence is the complete opposite of European painting. The divine light that falls down *from above* or emanates from a divine body, for instance, has a *blinding* effect. *Presence*, intensified into the divine, *blinds*.

In Vermeer's paintings, light often *falls into* the inside of a room. The gap formed by Vermeer's half-open window directs and bundles the light. Vermeer frequently lets light and darkness collide, which results in sharp contours that intensify presence. In *Girl with a Pearl Earring*, the shining white collar stands out against the dark background. Despite the intensity of Vermeer's light, it is, however, *not a blinding* light, because it does not have a transcendent source; its source is the *immanence* of the world and of things. Therefore, the light falling into the inside of the room does not appear *cold*. The peculiar warmth or mildness of Vermeer's light, in particular, points towards its origin in immanence. We could even say that Vermeer's things begin to shine *by them-*

36

selves. Things, such as buttons, earrings, collars or caps shine brightly without pointing towards an external source of light. This sourceless light appears to be *Eigenlicht*, a light inherent in the things, which seems to exist for the sole purpose of emphasizing their presence.

Vermeer's light is a light of *presencing*. It emphasizes the presence of things. The stationary light of shōji paper gives the appearance of a white layer of clouds that softly envelops the light.[4] It brings the light to a standstill, so to speak. Tanizaki Junichiro also admires this magic light of absence: 'We delight in the mere sight of the delicate glow of fading rays, clinging to the surface of a dusky wall, there to live out what little life remains to them.'[5] Shōji light is as restrained, as absencing, as the last glimmer of a dying light; the last glimmer, paradoxically, inscribes a *non-natural* vitality into the light. Because of its tenderness, shōji light is unable to *shine on* or *illuminate* the things in the room. The things thus retreat into an absence:

Illustration 7: Incidence of light

37

The little sunlight from the garden that manages to make its way beneath the eaves and through the corridors has by then lost its power to illuminate, seems drained of the complexion of life. It can do no more than accentuate the whiteness of the paper.[6]

The stationary light, which seems almost absent, does not harry the darkness. That is its friendliness. The heroic light that rigorously expels the darkness is not friendly. The friendly and restrained light of shōji paper, by contrast, creates an in-difference of brightness and darkness. A neither-bright-nor-dark, in-between light emerges, whose effect on Tanizaki Junichiro is

> as though some misty film were blunting my vision. The light from the pale white paper, powerless to dispel the heavy darkness of the alcove, is instead repelled by the darkness, creating a world of confusion where dark and light are indistinguishable.[7]

A dichotomy between light and shadow is unknown in the culture of the Far East. There, shadows have their own brilliance, and darkness is given its own brightness. Light and shadow, brightness and darkness, are not mutually exclusive. To the author of *In Praise of Shadows*, even yōkan (a dark-red Japanese confection made from red beans) appears to be a little gem made of glowing darkness:

> The cloudy translucence, like that of jade; the faint, dream-like glow that suffuses it, as if it had drunk into its very depths the light of the sun . . . And when yōkan is served in a lacquer dish within whose dark recesses its color is scarcely distinguishable, then it is most certainly an object for meditation. You take its cool, smooth substance into your mouth,

Illustration 8: Shōji: stationary light

and it is as if the very darkness of the room were melting on your tongue.[8]

Emptiness and absence also characterize the cuisine of the Far East. Rice, without a doubt the centre of Far Eastern cooking, appears empty because it lacks colour. The *centre is empty*. The bland taste of rice also pervades it with emptiness and absence. Zhuangzi would say that rice is able to cling to any dish, any taste, because it does not have a taste of its own. Rice appears as empty as the white ground of Far Eastern ink drawings. The small coloured bowls look like paint pots. In this way, the whole act of eating resembles painting. Rice is also empty at a tactile level. Cooked rice offers no resistance. Tempura, too, follows the principle of emptiness. It does not have the heaviness that typifies fried foods in Western cuisine. In tempura, the oil's only purpose is to turn the very thin layer of batter on the vegetables or fish into a crisp agglomeration of emptiness. The content within also acquires a delicious lightness. If, as in Korea, a tender green sesame leaf is used for tempura, it dissolves in the hot oil and turns into an almost bodiless, fragrant green. It is actually a pity that no cook has yet tried to use a tender green tea leaf for tempura. That would be a delicacy made up of the enchanting smell of tea and emptiness – a delicious dish of absence.

Far Eastern cuisine appears empty also because it does not have a centre. A Western visitor will find it hard to avoid the feeling that, despite the various little delicacies, there is something missing, without, however, being able to say what it is. The meals lack the centre or weight of a main dish and the *closedness* of a menu. This is probably also the reason why the menus of Chinese restaurants in the West differ from those in China itself. Far Eastern cuisine *disperses*, even *empties*, the main course, turning it into numerous small dishes that are served simultaneously.

In the Far East, eating is not a matter of cutting something up with knife and fork but a matter of putting something together with chopsticks. Western eating and thinking is disassembling, that is, analytical. However, it would be wrong to say that, by contrast, Eastern thinking and eating is synthetic. Analysis and synthesis belong to the same order. Far Eastern eating and thinking is neither analytic nor synthetic. Rather, it follows a *syndetic* order. Syndetic means connected, even *lined up*, by way of conjunction, an ongoing '*and*'. The categorical, the finality of a full stop or an exclamation mark, is unknown to Far Eastern thinking. It is rather determined by connecting commas and 'ands', by detours and side-tracks, or by concealed paths.

Ikebana is a Japanese art of flower arranging. 'Ikebana' literally means 'invigoration of the flower'. It is, however,

40

Illustration 9: Instructions of a Zen master in front of an Ikebana
in the 'literati style'

an unusual kind of invigoration, because the flower is cut off
from its root, from this natural organ of life, even of *appetitus*.
The flower is invigorated by dealing it a mortal blow. The
de-rooting step cuts off its *soul*, its *conatus ad Existentiam*, its
desire. This raises it above the process of slow withering,
its *natural* death. The flower is thereby removed from the
difference between 'life' and 'death'. It shines with a special
vitality, a flowering in-difference of 'life' and 'death' that has
its source in the *spirit* of emptiness. This is not the shining or
reflection of eternity but a shining of absence. In the midst of
radical transience, the flower radiates a vitality that is non- or
un-natural, a *duration* that does not *endure*.

Japanese rock gardens are gardens of absence and emptiness. No flower, no tree, no trace of humans can be seen in
them. Despite this emptiness and absence, they radiate an
intense vitality that is owed to multiple counter-movements.
The flow of the wave lines raked into the gravel contrasts

41

with the calm of the rocks. The darkness of the rocks forms a silhouette against the whiteness of the gravel. The horizontal rivers and the vertical mountains, the circular lines of the water and the ragged lines of the rocks, create further tension through counter-movement. The counter-movement implies a turning point, a breathturn [Atemwende] at a point of in-difference. In 'The Sutra of Mountains and Water', Zen master Dōgen says:

> Never insult them [i.e. the mountains] by saying that the Blue Mountains cannot walk or that the East Mountain cannot move on water. It is because of the grossness of the viewpoint of the vulgar that they doubt the phrase 'the Blue Mountains are walking'. It is due to the poorness of their scant experience that they are astonished at the words 'flowing mountains'.⁹

The rock garden is another realization of the method of paradoxical invigoration. It invigorates nature by completely *drying out* its *soul*, its *conatus ad Existentiam*. Nature's natural and organic desire is killed. The Zen garden made of stone, this place of *sur-vival*, puts nature into a state of *satori*. It *spiritualizes* nature by cutting off nature's *soul*. Raised above 'life' and 'death', nature shines in emptiness and absence.

'Bunraku' is the name for the Japanese puppet theatre. It has little in common with Western puppet theatre, though. In a Bunraku theatre, the puppets are led neither by strings nor by invisible hands, which would gesture towards an inevitable fate or hidden God. The puppets, between one and two metres tall, are moved by three *visible* actors on the stage, a master and his two helpers, all dressed in black. The faces of the helpers are covered by a black scarf. The faces of the masters, by contrast, are not covered, but they remain empty, without any expression, as if they had no *soul*. The Western

Illustration 10: Garden of absencing

puppet theatre *animates* the soulless with the help of voices
and movements. This process of animation is fascinating.
The theatre of absencing, by contrast, is not a *theatre of the
soul*. The puppets of Bunraku therefore have no *voice of their
own*, the voice being the medium of the soul and of animation. Significance is reduced to gestures. Instead of voices
belonging to souls, one hears reciters who sit, immobile,
while presenting, in a half singing tone, the text in front of
them. Their presentation, however, is not a *chant*, not a *song*.
It is as *dry* as the rock gardens. In the theatre of absencing,
emotional states, such as mourning or wrath, also lose their
character as expressions of the soul. They do not seem to
be offshoots or twitches of the soul. Rather, they *de-inter-
nalize* or *de-animate* themselves and become mere *figures*.
The *cathartic effect* of the play is brought about especially by

this abstraction or *figuralization*, which is another kind of *desiccation*.

A stage of absence unfolds in front of the audience. Noh theatre is also a theatre of absence. The stiff silk costumes and empty masks make the actors look like puppets. As in the rock gardens, the *soul* is *dried up*. Whenever an actor appears without a mask, the uncovered face is expressionless and empty. The narrative composition of a Noh play also contributes to the atmosphere of absence. The basic narrative model is the mutual penetration of dream and reality. Reality is shrouded in dream-like hovering. Things appear, only to disappear into absence again. The ghostly figures from the past and the only loosely connected elements of the plot create a temporal in-difference. The sliding steps of the actors intensify the effect of dream-like hovering. Dream and reality flow into each other. In this world of absence and in-difference, it is very difficult to see where dream ends and reality begins.

Illustrations 11 and 12: Noh: theatre without souls

Knowledge and Daftness –
On the Way to Paradise

the sun's path –
hollyhocks turn with it
in summer rains
Bashō[1]

Some passages of Kleist's 'On the Marionette Theatre' read like one of Zhuangzi's wondrous stories. 'Herr C.', who seems to be familiar with quite a few of the world's secrets, behaves like a Daoist sage. He admires in particular the graceful movements of the marionettes. His theory is that their grace is attributable to the fact that they lack a soul, that, like artificial limbs, they follow purely mechanical, purely physical laws:

Have you, he asked while I gazed thoughtfully at the ground, ever heard of those mechanical legs that English craftsmen manufacture for unfortunate people who have lost their own limbs?

I replied that I had never seen such artifacts.

That's a shame, he replied, for when I tell you that these unfortunate people are able to dance with the use of them, you most certainly will not believe me. What do I mean by using the word dance? The span of their movements is quite limited, but those movements of which they are capable are accomplished with a composure, lightness, and grace that would amaze any thinking mind.[2]

'On the Marionette Theatre' could just as well be titled 'De Anima'. In it, Kleist presents a specific psychology. The soul is held responsible for human dancers' lack of grace. The human dancer, that is, the dancer with a soul, tries *consciously* to steer the body. But human consciousness is imperfect. It is constantly off the mark:

> Take for example the dancer P., he continued. When she dances Daphne and is pursued by Apollo, she looks back at him – her soul is located in the vertebrae of the small of her back; she bends as if she were about to break in half . . . And look at the young dancer F. When he dances Paris and stands among the three goddesses and hands the apple to Venus, his soul is located precisely in his elbow, and it is a frightful thing to behold.[3]

Herr C. derives the grace of the marionettes from their non-doing [Nichts-Tun]. 'Without anyone's aid' [ohne irgendein Zutun], the text says, the marionettes follow 'the simple law of gravity'.[4] When moved along a simple line, the limbs, without being individually directed by the puppeteer, and as if moving *all by themselves*, follow complex curves. And if 'simply shaken in an arbitrary manner, the whole figure assumed a kind of rhythmic movement'.[5] This suggests a comparison with Zhuangzi's theory of idleness. Like water effortlessly

46

flowing down a valley, the marionettes make use of the potential of gravity inherent in a situation. They do nothing, but allow themselves to be moved by the law of gravity. A human dancer, by contrast, intentionally and consciously tries to set *himself* in motion. He always does *too much*. This *doing too much* deprives his movement of grace. However, such a 'Daoist' interpretation of the text fails at a crucial point, for the marionettes are 'anti-gravitational':

> In addition, he went on, these puppets possess the virtue of being anti-gravitational. They know nothing of the inertia of matter, that quality which above all is diametrically opposed to the dance, because the force that lifts them into the air is greater than the one that binds them to the earth. What wouldn't our good G. give to be sixty pounds lighter, or to use a force of this weight to assist her with her entrechats and pirouettes? Like elves, the puppets need only to touch upon the ground, and the soaring of their limbs is newly animated through this momentary hesitation; we dancers need the ground to rest upon and recover from the exertion of the dance.[6]

The marionettes may be soulless 'matter', but as the text has it, they 'know nothing of the inertia of matter'. Thus, they are not mere matter after all. The strings with the help of which the divine puppeteer directs them take the inertia of matter away from them; in a certain sense, they even give them wings. If they were pure matter, they would not be anti-gravitational. They would, like all matter, be subjected to weight and inertia. They are anti-gravitational because of the *vertical* force that originates above and is 'greater' than the gravitational force that 'binds' them to the earth.

The anti-gravitational desire of Kleist's dancers does not animate the Far East. The Far East's dances know of neither high jumps nor quick pirouettes. The Korean monk's dance (*sung-mu*), which translates emptiness and absence into movement, follows long, mostly horizontal lines at an extremely slow speed. The fundamental movement of Noh dancing is also a sliding step. The dancers slide along the ground with their toes raised only slightly. There are no vertical movements. There is no heroic anti-gravity to disrupt the horizontal line. In contrast to the sliding Noh dancers, Kleist's puppets *hover* above the ground, thanks to the vertical force that pulls them up. The strings connect them with God, with the divine puppeteer. The puppets are divine limbs, so to speak, de-materialized matter. Thus, when Kleist juxtaposes the puppet, as pure matter, with God, the argument is not quite coherent:

> I replied that although he handled his paradoxes with skill, he would never convince me that in a mechanical figure there could be more grace than in the structure of the human body.
>
> He replied that it would be almost impossible for a man to attain even an approximation of a mechanical being. In such a realm only a God could measure up to this matter, and this is the point where both ends of the circular world would join one another.[7]

Anti-gravity is the fundamental characteristic of the *Western soul*, even of Western thinking. To Hegel, journeying through the Bernese Oberland, the mountains appeared as 'eternally dead masses', and they offered him 'nothing but the unchanging and at length boring . . . idea: this is how it is (es ist so)'.[8] Hegel is bored by the inertia and heaviness of matter, and the 'eternal noise' of a glacial river cascading over a rocky bed also provokes in him a deep boredom: 'in the end, however, all this elicits boredom in a person not used to it and walking alongside it for multiple hours'.[9] The Staubbach Falls at Lauterbrunnen, by contrast, Hegel likes. Delighted by the sight of it, he notes in his diary:

> But the graceful unforced free play of this water vapour has something all the more precious about it . . . one's mind does not turn to the coercion, to the *must of nature* . . . and instead the lively, the constantly dissolving, disintegrating . . . that which eternally moves forward and is active produces the image of free play.[10]

As such, Staubbach Falls is also soulless, but its *rising* water vapour gives the impression of a soul, that is, of *anti-gravity*. Anti-gravity is the fundamental trait of Hegel's 'spirit'. The semblance of 'free play', of what 'eternally moves forward and is active', gives the illusion of spirit. The anti-gravity of the water, the quasi-spirituality of this soulless matter, clearly fascinated Hegel.

Herr C. remarks that one must have read the third chapter of Genesis carefully in order to understand him. That chapter, of course, is about the fall. The consumption of the fruit of the tree of knowledge gives human beings a consciousness that is able to *distinguish* between good and evil; that is, it gives them the *capacity to distinguish* as such. But this human consciousness is finite. Herr C. explains all human inadequacies in terms of human finitude. Human consciousness introduces order, but it causes disorder. It clarifies, but it does not reach complete transparency and does not establish all evidence. It directs, but at the same time distracts: 'I told him that I understood only too well how consciousness creates disorder in the natural harmony of men.'[11] Consciousness grasps [greift] and understands [begreift], but it constantly goes amiss [vergreift sich]. 'Such mistakes [Mißgriffe], he mused, cutting himself short, are inevitable because we have eaten of the tree of knowledge. And Paradise is bolted, with the cherub behind us.'[12]

For Kleist, the way out of human Dasein's awkwardness, namely, the possibility of regaining grace, can be sought only through an intensification of the power of knowledge and reflection. Knowledge and consciousness need to become infinite:

Now, my excellent friend, said Herr C., you are in possession of everything that is necessary to comprehend what I am saying. We can see the degree to which contemplation becomes darker and weaker in the organic world, so that the grace that is there emerges all the more shining and triumphant. Just as the intersection of two lines from the same side of a point after passing through the infinite suddenly finds itself again on the other side – or as the image from a concave mirror, after having gone off into the infinite, suddenly appears before us again – so grace returns after knowledge has gone through the world of the infinite, in that it appears to best advantage in that human bodily structure that has no consciousness at all – or has infinite consciousness – that is, in the mechanical puppet, or in the God.

Therefore, I replied, somewhat at loose ends, we would have to eat again of the tree of knowledge to fall back again into a state of innocence?[13]

Kleist's anecdote follows the fundamental schema of Western metaphysical thinking. For Plato, the 'soul' strives towards the divine, the infinite. In its anti-gravitational nature, it is an organ of desire. Its feathered wings allow it to shed its heaviness and float upwards towards the gods: 'By their nature wings have the power to lift up heavy things and raise them aloft where the gods all dwell.'[14] Kleist consistently thinks in terms of the dichotomy between consciousness and

50

matter, spirit and body, subject and object, activity and passivity. The world is in the first place something resistant that must be broken down by raising consciousness to a more intense level. The virtuoso must *break* the inertia of matter by maximizing his activity. The idea of virtuosity also adheres to a dichotomous schema. The object is *mastered*, its resistance broken down by intensifying subjective activity. The dancer is an active subject who *masters* his body. His *skill* and *capability* make him a *master*. Grace is the result of such *domination*. By means of the effort and exertion of the subject, the body is *dominated*. The notion of 'virtuosity' is derived from *virtus* (virtue). Its moral substance is mainly a *striving for* or *striving against*. The idea of virtuosity is essentially anti-gravitational.

Far Eastern thinking, by contrast, is pro-gravitational. Across different philosophical schools there is agreement that one should accommodate oneself to the *naturally* given things and give *oneself* up, forget oneself in favour of the regularities of worldly immanence. In particular, this thinking raises itself above the sphere of subjectivity, above the dichotomous relation between matter and spirit. Far Eastern thinking is pro-gravitational insofar as it seeks to accommodate itself to the *weight of the world*. It teaches that resistance emerges only through striving. To adapt Kleist's words, we could say: the darker and weaker reflection becomes, the more the *grace of the world*, the *grace of things*, begins to shine and come to the fore. The pro-gravitational makes the immanence of the world radiate in its gracefulness and natural order, which are pushed aside where consciousness comes to the fore. Zhuangzi would say that, instead of eating once again from the tree of knowledge, one should undo the first consumption of its fruit.

In response to Herr C., Zhuangzi would tell the story of a very forgetful man who forgets to walk when he is out and about, and forgets to sit when he is at home,[15] or the story of the woodworker who forgets even his body and limbs (*wang wu you si zhi xing ti ye*, 忘吾有四肢形體也) but therefore has the ability immediately to grasp the natural properties (*tian xing*, 天性) of a tree. His conclusion is: 'This way I am simply matching up "Heaven" with "Heaven". That's probably the reason that people wonder if the results were not made by spirits.'[16] The weaker consciousness and the power of reflection become, the more brightly the things reveal themselves. In other words, less power of reflection means more world. Zhuangzi repeatedly invokes absence and forgetting. The sage is 'absent and soulless' (*mo ran wu hun*, 莫然無魂).[17] He is 'like a fool, like a man without consciousness' (*ruo yu ruo hun*, 若愚若昏).[18] The most perfect horse 'seems absent, he seems to have become unaware of his own identity' (*ruo xu ruo shi*, 若卹若失).[19] 'To forget all things and to forget heaven, that is called being oblivious of self. But whoever is oblivious of self reaches heaven for that very reason' (*wang hu wu, wang hu tian, qi ming wei wang ji, wang ji zhi ren, shi zhi wei ru yu tian*, 忘乎物 忘乎天 其名為忘己 忘己之人 是之謂入於天).[20] A good ruler does not govern the state with knowledge (*zhi*, 智) but through foolishness (*yu*, 愚).[21] Instead of foolishness one could also say *daftness*, because 'daft' originally meant 'mild', 'meek' or 'timid'. It is a sensibility for phenomena that transcend the dimension of consciousness and reflection, the level of intention and will.

The relationship with the world is not dominated by the decisiveness of doing and acting, or by the clarity of consciousness and reflection. Rather, one lets the world happen, lets oneself be filled with it by retreating into an absence, by being oblivious of self or by emptying oneself, like a chamber whose emptiness means it can be filled with light and become bright (*xu shi sheng bai*, 虛室生白).[22] Rather than decisive action, what is sought is something unforced, a kind of effortlessness. This is probably the Far Eastern counterpart to the

Western notion of freedom. But as opposed to the idea of freedom, which is ultimately based on a world-less subject, effortlessness is the result of an in-difference between consciousness and world, between inside and outside. The body is neither something to be dominated nor a means for expressing the soul or subjectivity. Even though the body should be given a proper posture (*ruo zheng ru xing*, 若正汝形),[23] this working on the body only serves the purpose of opening it up, making it permeable for the heavenly vital force that animates, renews, harmonizes and pacifies the entire world (*tian he jiang zhi*, 天和將至).

'Virtuosity' is not something possessed by the famous poet Tao Yuanming, who according to one story played a stringless zither (*qin*). Without any strings to pluck, virtuosity and dexterity are superfluous. Strings are even an obstacle to great music, because such music is without sound (*da yin xi sheng*, 大音希聲).[24] Strings would determine what resists all determination. However, strings and sounds are not renounced in the interests of the 'sublime', the 'absolute essence' of music or some divine 'transcendence' that *flees* from sound. Strings and sounds are not discarded because of a '*not enough*' but because of a '*too much*'. Too much doing and presence rigidifies and fixes what otherwise would be an endless process. Tao Yuanming's fingers do not play of their own accord. At best, they follow the heavenly chord. The main reason Yuanming does not display virtuosity is that he does not exert himself, does not do anything, does not try to master anything. Virtuosity, after all, is based on maximizing activity. If anything, Tao Yuanming would be a virtuoso of doing nothing.

The wondrous music of the 'Yellow Emperor' suspends all separations and boundaries. Because it does so, it first causes fear and timidity (*ju*, 懼), followed by tiredness and exhaustion (*dai*, 怠). Then it leads to confusion (*huo*, 惑), and finally it produces a feeling of being daft (*yu*, 愚). One loses oneself amid the tranquillity of unboundedness (*dang dang mo mo, nai bu zi de*, 蕩蕩默默乃不自得).[25] Tiredness and daftness open up wide spaces of absencing. They allow the I to retreat, in favour of a *world*. The heavenly play of an organ (*tian lai*, 天籟) makes Master Ziqi absent and oblivious of self (*da yan*, 荅焉). When his worried pupil asks about his state, he says that he has lost his self (*sang wo*, 喪我).[26]

Knowledge needs to give way to forgetting. Forgetting, however, is an utmost affirmation. 'You forget your feet', Zhuangzi says, 'when the shoes are comfortable. You forget your waist when the belt is comfortable.'[27] This implies that forgetting is based on an agreement that allows for non-resistance and non-coercion. You *forget your head*, Zhuangzi's image could be extended, when you think in the right way. You even forget *yourself*, when you *fully* are. Complete harmony reigns where you even forget about the right way of being (*wang shi zhi shi ye*, 忘適之適也).[28]

Zhuangzi's demand that one let go of knowledge and insight (*qu zhi*, 去知)[29] is the direct opposite of Herr C.'s belief that the only way to leave the misery of human existence behind is to maximize knowledge. For Herr C., humans are doomed because they have not eaten enough of the tree of knowledge. Endowed with only finite consciousness, they are expelled from paradise. They can be saved, even redeemed, by achieving infinite consciousness, by eating of the tree of knowledge once again. But paradise is bolted. And the cherub, his wings spread, guards the heavenly gate. Kleist therefore concludes: 'we must journey around the world and determine if perhaps at the end somewhere there is an opening to be discovered again'.[30] We can rule out the possibility that on the journey around the world some unlocked back-door to paradise will be discovered. But maybe the travellers will unexpectedly end up in a foreign, unheard-of land called

'China', which is paradisiacal or utopian in its own way, a land of absence and forgetting, where you forget to walk when out and about, and you forget to sit when at home, where singers forget to sing and dancers forget to dance.

Land and Sea – Strategies of Thinking

Establish the love of the towers that dominate the sands.[1]
Antoine de Saint-Exupéry, *Citadelle*

The maritime adventure is a popular metaphor in Western philosophical thought. Conquering stormy seas is seen as a heroic undertaking. The world appears in the form of a resistance that has to be broken through determined action. For instance, Hegel compares thinking to an adventurous journey on an *'endless ocean'*, where 'all the bright colours, all footholds, have disappeared, all other friendly lights are extinguished'. In the face of this vast oceanic expanse and uncertainty, the mind 'is seized by horror'.[2]

Hegel's geo-philosophical remarks on the sea and seafaring resemble an allegorical description of Greco-Western thinking. 'The sea', Hegel says, must be confronted with 'cunning', 'wisdom' and 'courage', because one is dealing here with the most 'cunning', with the 'most unreliable and deceitful element'. The sea's surface is 'absolutely yielding – withstanding no pressure, not even a breath of wind', so 'it looks bound-lessly innocent, submissive, friendly, and supple'. But 'it is exactly this submissiveness which changes the sea into the most dangerous and violent element', and this is what makes the sea so deceitful. Hegel is apparently unable to dwell on the positive properties of water, such as submissiveness, sup-pleness or friendliness, and to see in them the possibility of a *friendly, supple thinking*. He very quickly blames the submis-siveness of the sea for its violence. The sea's friendliness is deceitful:

> To this deceitfulness and violence man opposes merely a simple piece of wood; confides entirely in his courage and presence of mind; and thus passes from a firm ground to an unstable support [ein Haltungsloses], taking his artificial ground with him. The Ship – that swan of the sea, which cuts the watery plain in agile and arching movements or describes circles upon it – is a machine whose invention does the greatest honor to the boldness of man as well as to his understanding.[7]

It is possible that at the sight of water the idea occurred to Hegel that water as such is mendacious because it perma-nently changes its form, because it does not have a form *of its own* at all, because it never resembles *itself*, because it lacks all permanence. Hegel seems to have seen water as a counter-figure to *truth*. Land does not yield, and it offers resistance to pressure. It offers a solid ground [Halt], whereas the sea rep-resents 'an unstable support' [das Haltungslose]. Land also has a solid form. Permanence, an important ingredient of essence, is proper to it. Hegel's perception of water and the sea is everywhere guided by a compulsive desire for solidity. Only because of this preoccupation with solidity does the sea appear to be 'an unstable support', the 'most unreliable' element.

57

Kant also uses the metaphor of seafaring as an illustration of his thinking. As opposed to Hume, who 'deposited his ship on the beach (of skepticism) for safekeeping, where it could then lie and rot', he wants to give his ship a helmsman who 'might safely navigate the ship wherever seems good to him, following sound principles of the helmsman's art drawn from a knowledge of the globe'.[4] The Kantian art of helmsmanship conquers the sea by framing it with a system of principles and fully charting it with fixed coordinates. Western thinking has its source in a desire for a solid ground. It is precisely this compulsive desire for permanence and clarity that makes every deviation, every transformation, look like a threat.

If 'reason', as the 'ultimate touchstone of truth', sets sail for the beyond of objective intuition, it ends up in a dark space.[5] It has to find orientation 'in the immeasurable space of the supra-sensory realm which we see as full of utter darkness'.[6] Reason follows the 'feeling of a need' to make judgements, and if reason is to be 'satisfied', it requires a *maxim* that provides a *maximum* of consistency and generality.[7] Reason must illuminate the abysmal darkness. If we look more closely, this 'utter darkness' is not a matter of *facticity*. It is the product of a compulsion. Only with the imperative of truth are all friendly lights extinguished. The more coercive this imperative becomes, the darker the night will be. Only with the compulsion to establish a fixed order does water appear to be an unstable support, to be indeterminate and deceitful. Its suppleness and friendliness are no longer perceived.

For Heidegger, Kant is a 'genuine' thinker insofar as he looked into the shallows and the abyss of being. According to Heidegger, thinking loves the abyss. Thinking is the result of a 'lucid courage for essential anxiety'.[8] The beginning of thinking is not trust in the world but anxiety. Thus, thinking bravely exposes itself to the 'silent voice that attunes us to the horror of the abyss'.[9] Heidegger also uses the metaphor of the abysmal sea to which thinking must expose itself. During his journey through Greece, he thinks of Pindar, who is supposed to have called Crete the 'wave-taming island' and 'the fatherland of the skilful rowers'.[10] Presumably, thinking therefore also has to tame the wild waves, for it moves 'on the billowing waters of an ocean'[11] and in the 'abyss of the waves of the ocean'.[12]

The image of the mind as a 'swan of the sea', battling the endless ocean on a 'simple piece of wood' as its 'artificial ground', cannot be found in Chinese thinking. Zhuangzi also talks about ships and the sea. But the *proportions* are different. In the first section, Zhuangzi tells a story about a dark sea in the barren north. In it lives a giant fish that turns into a giant bird whose wings span several thousand *li*. The size of this creature sets it apart from the small, helpless swan of the sea. And this sea, not least because of the size of the creatures that populate it, has nothing threatening about it. The relationship with the sea is governed by an altogether different perspective. Zhuangzi remarks that only a leaf of grass can swim in a puddle, that shallow water cannot carry a large ship (*shui qian er zhou da*, 水淺而舟大).[13] Only a deep sea can carry it and get it moving. Likewise, the giant bird Peng first ascends to a great height so that the strong winds can carry it to the 'southern darkness'.[14] Because of the bird's size, the strong winds cannot harm it. It *floats* on them. A weak wind would not have the power to carry its *giant* wings (*feng zhi ji ye bu hou, ze qi fu da yi ye wu li*, 風之積也不厚 則其負大翼也無力).[15] An interesting reversal of the relation between small and great takes place here. The mind is not a swan of the sea that has to conquer the enormous, hostile ocean. Rather, the mind is as *great*, as *all-encompassing*, as the sea. The mind unites with all of the sea. If the mind *is* the sea, the sea poses no threat. The all-encompassing mind is not caught by powerful winds. Rather, it seeks strong winds in order to rise to great heights.

The inhabitants of Zhuangzi's world are often of an unimaginable size. There is a fisherman who fixes fifty oxen as bait to his angling rod and throws the line out into the eastern sea while perching on a high hill. The fish he catches is gigantic; enormous white waves swell when it whips the water with its fins, and the seawater turns to foam. Zhuangzi also tells of a tree whose spring and autumn each last eight thousand years. The tree is compared to a little cicada that lives only one summer and does not know spring or autumn. The tree completely transcends the cicada's imagination, and thus it does not understand the tree. Then there is the story of a giant tree that is too gnarled, bent and misshapen to be of any use. Zhuangzi asks Huizi, who recognizes its uselessness, why he does not stroll idly around under the tree or lie down for a sleep in its shadow. And a big yak covering the sky is juxtaposed to a small weasel that carelessly frolics around and chases mice until it dies itself in one of the mouse traps. Zhuangzi's words are themselves so big that they seem useless (*da er wu yong*, 大而無用). They advance without returning (*wang er bu fan*, 往而不反) and cannot be pinned down. There is also talk of a gigantic gourd. Huizi complains that it is too big to be used as a spoon and dipped into things, and Zhuangzi tells him that his ignorance means he still does not know how to deal with what is great. He asks Huizi why he did not think of making it into a great tub, so that he could go floating around in rivers and lakes. Zhuangzi's conclusion is that small knowledge does not reach up to large knowledge (*xiao zhi bu ji da zhi*, 小知不及大知).[16]

It is problematic when Richard Wilhelm calls Zhuangzi's giant fish *Kun* a 'Leviathan'. This biblical name suggests ideas that do not at all fit into Zhuangzi's world. The sea monster of the Old Testament revolts against God and His creation.

In the Old Testament's world of ideas, the sea symbolizes the hostile power that threatens God's order.[17] The name 'Leviathan' thus evokes ideas of creation and chaos that are wholly alien to Chinese thinking. The giant fish has very little in common with the violent, deadly and unpredictable sea monsters of the Greek world. They are occasionally also associated with knowledge and wisdom, but of a kind shrouded in mystery and riddles. The metamorphoses of Proteus, for instance, serve the purpose of *hiding* his knowledge. *Withdrawal* [Entzug] is a trait of his nature [Wesenszug]. Only cunning and violence are able to wrest his knowledge from him.[18] The knowledge promised by the Sirens is also shrouded in mystery and riddles.[19] It neighbours death. Even Heraclitus, although he renounces being in favour of becoming, remains a Greek thinker insofar as he believes that nature loves to hide. Chinese wisdom, by contrast, does not hide. It does not withdraw and is not shrouded in mystery. Instead, it is placed under the light of a particular kind of evidence, of the obviousness of *being-so*, of a *bright being-present*.

The intention behind Zhuangzi's use of entities of such extraordinary dimensions is not to create a feeling of the sublime, that feeling caused by an object whose proportions the imagination cannot grasp. Kant calls '*sublime* what is *absolutely* [*schlechthin*] *large*' (*absolute, non comparative magnum*), what is '*large beyond all comparison*'.[20] The feeling of the sublime arises when an object's size exceeds the power of the imagination for the sensuous judgement of dimensions. In such cases, the imagination is unable to capture the object in an image. In failing to create a representation, it is led beyond itself to a different kind of cognitive faculty, namely reason. Reason, because it does not depend on sensuality, is capable of forming ideas, for instance the idea of the infinite. The feeling of the sublime results from the antagonism between imagination and reason, between the

61

sensory and the supra-sensory. It emerges the very moment the sensory is exceeded towards the supra-sensory. It is a vertical feeling, always a feeling of transcendence. It results from the tension between immanence and transcendence, between phenomenon and noumenon. The excessively large dimensions of Zhuangzi's things, by contrast, do not lead to anything supra-sensory or to the 'idea' of the infinite. They do not end in the demand 'to estimate any sense object in nature that is large for us as being small when compared with ideas of reason'.[21] Rather, Zhuangzi's strategy is to use these over-sized things to unbound, de-substantialize and de-differentiate. To be large means to raise oneself above rigid distinctions and oppositions, above all final assumptions, even to de-differentiate oneself into an *impartial friendliness*. Someone who is as *big as the world* will not be hindered or impeded by anything *in* the world. Someone who does not *reside in* the world, and instead unbounds and expands himself to encompass the world, does not know of any hither and thither, up and down; he has no recollection or expectation, no joy or disgust, no affection or aversion. Being-in-the-world has to give way to being-world. That is the meaning of hiding 'the world in the world' (*zang tian xia yu tian xia*, 藏天下於天下).[22] Being large removes 'Dasein' (Heidegger) from its structure of care [Sorge-Struktur]. It leads to a de-caring [Ent-Sorgung]. Zhuangzi's first section, in which his giant creatures abound, treats precisely of the carefree, of 'free and easy wandering' (*xiao yao you*, 逍遙遊). It discusses a special kind of *effortlessness*, which is the Far Eastern counterpart to the Western concept of 'freedom'. You are effortless when you do not set anything against the world, when you fully unite with it.

Hegel remarks that China does not have a positive relationship with the sea, despite bordering on it. For the Chinese, he says, the sea is only 'the ceasing of the land'.[23] In fact, the Chinese have a very positive relationship with the sea. However, for them, the transition from land to sea is not a transition from 'a firm ground to an unstable support' that gives rise to an adventurous spirit or a feeling of terror.[24] Chinese thinking involves an altogether different relationship to the world; it is characterized by a deep trust in the world.

Section seventeen of Zhuangzi is titled 'Autumn Floods', a treatise about water and sea. It consists of conversations between the holy god of the river and the holy god of the sea, in which the latter plays the role of the sage, or knowledgeable one. The section begins thus:

> The time of the autumn floods came, and the hundred streams poured into the Yellow River. Its racing current swelled to such proportions that, looking from bank to bank or island to island, it was impossible to distinguish a horse from a cow. Then the Lord of the River was beside himself with joy, believing that all the beauty in the world belonged to him alone.[25]

Because of the flooded riverbanks, the ox on one side cannot be distinguished from the horse on the other side (*bu bian niu mu*, 不辨牛馬). It is interesting that the swelling water, which makes differences disappear, is not seen as a threat. Rather, the fact that ox and horse cannot be distinguished from each other, that things flow into each other, is beautiful. It is not the clear separation but the transition towards in-difference that is beautiful.

> The sea darkening
> a wild duck's call
> faintly white
>> Bashō[26]

63

In the Far East, water and sea occupy entirely different semantic fields. They are symbols for very different processes and relations. They often figure as mediums of in-difference. Water is in-different insofar as it does not have a form *of its own*. It has no inwardness. It is therefore opposed to *essences*, which assert *themselves*, which by remaining *within themselves* distinguish themselves from what is other and resist it. Water may not have a form *of its own*, but it is anything but 'amorphous'. It always has a shape, because it takes the form of the other in order to unfold. It is friendly because, instead of positing, positing itself, it snuggles up to any form. Because it lacks all solidity, water does not exercise any coercion. It is yielding and flexible. Thus, it does not encounter any resistance. As it does not assert *itself*, does not resist anything, does not oppose anything, it does not compete in strife (*bu zheng*, 不爭). Thus, 'the highest goodness is like water' (*shang shan ruo shui*, 上善若水).[27] As it is nothing, has no fixed form, no inwardness, even is *ab-sencing*, it can be everywhere and everything. What is hard can easily break; it provokes resistance. The one who exercises coercion will suffer coercion. Water overcomes obstacles by giving in. It unfolds by succumbing. Laozi says: 'Water overcomes rock; soft overcomes firm' (*ruo zhi sheng qiang, rou zhi sheng gang*, 弱之勝強 柔之勝剛).[28]

The sea symbolizes the *world's immanent space of in-difference*, out of which the contours of things emerge and into which they flow back again. A formative force is inherent to this space, but this formative force does not lead to ultimate distinctions or rigid oppositions. Asked by the river god whether heaven and earth should be called huge and the tip of a hair small, the god of the sea answers:

No indeed! . . . There is no end to the weighing of things, no stop to time, no constancy to the division of lots, no fixed rule to beginning and end. Therefore great wisdom observes

64

both far and near, and for that reason, it recognizes small without considering it paltry, recognizes large without considering it unwieldy, for it knows that there is no end to the weighing of things.[29]

Old Chinese is itself a language of in-difference, a flowing language, a language of flowing. It is extremely supple and rich in transitions, intermediary levels and combinations. The grammatical value of Old Chinese signs cannot be unambiguously defined. They are situated on a continuum. Some signs exhibit a strong tendency towards a certain grammatical function. But most signs exhibit a great deal of flexibility. The sign *da* (*large*, 大), for example, can be used as a verb, adjective, noun or adverb. It is not unusual for a sign to hover between grammatical possibilities. The grammatical value of a sign is not a fixed *property* of the sign. Rather, it is the result of its relations, that is, the context. The grammatical value of a sign is therefore not immediately visible on its surface. The meanings of Old Chinese signs are also not unambiguous. The sign *wei* (為) oscillates between a transitive and intransitive meaning, between active and passive. The sign *er* (而) means 'and' or 'then' as well as 'but'. It marks a transition, a joint, a switching point, so to speak, without the direction being fixed.

Essences produce not only a deep tension between inwardness and externality but also a lateral tension between identity and difference. They help the One to distinguish itself from the Other, while remaining fully within itself. Solid contours delineate an essence. Emptiness is the counter-figure to such an essence [Wesen]. Emptiness *absences* [verabwest] the world. Old Chinese is a language of emptiness and absencing. Its signs are highly mobile elements that do not, as such, possess any essential traits. Only within a specific constellation do they acquire an identity. When they are removed from their position, they return to their state of in-difference.

In Old Chinese, signs without a fixed lexical identity are called 'empty signs' (*xu ci*, 虛辭). They are particles that function like binding or lubricating linguistic elements that ensure the composition or atmosphere of a sentence (*yu qi*, 語氣). They contribute significantly to the flexibility and plasticity of Old Chinese. Without them, the language would solidify into rigid, one-dimensional structures. It is interesting that they are called 'empty' signs. The expression 'empty', *xu*, does not mean that they *lack* meaning. It is not a negation. Rather, something positive is associated with it. Water is also empty because it does not have a form of its own. But precisely because of this emptiness, it can carry, move and animate everything. The empty signs are like water, without a form of their own.

Old Chinese also makes a distinction between living (*huo zi*, 活字) and dead signs (*si zi*, 死字). Dead are those signs that express a state of being in nominal or adjectival form. Living, by contrast, are those signs that express a process in the form of verbs. Living words (*huo ju*, 活句) are also those expressions that deviate from conventional rules, that open themselves up to special semantic constellations. Words that permit only one meaning, by contrast, are called dead words (*si ju*, 死句). The Chinese experience what is identical, unchanging, what is insistent and lasting, as dead. Transformations and changes, transitions and states of in-difference, by contrast, are affirmed as alive and animating. In the Far Eastern sensibility in general, *vitality* is not seen as a force of insistence but as a force of transformation and change. *Light*, which comes up so often in Western thinking, is not able to transport this vitality. Light, as an element, may not be as solid as land, but there is a rigidity to it. The vitality in question corresponds precisely to the properties of water. This is why the figure

66

of water returns again and again in Far Eastern thinking. By contrast, terms such as 'ground' or 'foundation', which suggest insistence, do not belong to the vocabulary of Far Eastern thinking.

In Old Chinese, signs that are frequently surrounded by an uncertain semantic penumbra, even an in-difference, are combined according to a very subtle logic that can be put into a set of grammatical rules only with great difficulty. As opposed to Western languages, in which words are chained together, so to speak, without any possibility for deviation, the signs of Old Chinese have in-between spaces that make them very flexible. The empty in-between spaces, even spaces of in-difference, make it harder to establish the signs' meaning or grammatical value without ambiguity, but they afford the language an elegance and vitality. Old Chinese has a special style and aesthetic. The ellipses and omissions create beautiful and elegant effects. Old Chinese shines with a cryptic or telegraphic brevity. It is, however, a cryptography without secret, and a telegraphy without haste. Only what is essential is expressed. Thus, poetry and economy coincide in Old Chinese. It is a style that speaks in intermediate tones, even intermediate meanings, that opens itself up for transitions instead of drawing sharp boundaries, that does not subsume but lists, that permits a flowing instead of fixating and pinning down. This makes it a graceful style.

In Old Chinese, the meaning and grammatical value of a sign result only from the sign's position within the structure of a sentence. They are not steady properties of a sign. Likewise, Chinese thinking does not imbue things with an unchanging nature. The things behave like empty signs. They are not the carriers of a substance. Rather, they are *for themselves ab-sencing* or *in-different*. Only as part of a particular constellation do they assume an identity, a specific character. It is no coincidence that the signs without fixed meaning are called 'empty'. Emptiness is a theme in Chinese thinking. Daoist emptiness, *xu* (虛), resembles an extreme form of the empty sign, even the emptiest of signs, which, out of its state of in-difference, can take on any grammatical form, can transform itself into any other sign.

Zhuangzi calls the state of in-difference *hundun* (渾沌).[30] Interestingly, the left sides of both the sign *hun* (渾) and the sign *dun* (沌) refer to water. The personified *Hundun* inhabits the 'middle' (*zhong yang*, 中央) between the South and North Sea.[31] He is very hospitable towards the emperors of the North Sea, *Shu*, and of the South Sea, *Hu*, and they wonder how they may repay his kindness. As he does not have any bodily openings for seeing, hearing, eating or breathing, they decide that they will equip him with them. Every day, they bore a hole, and on the seventh day *Hundun* dies. This anecdote says a lot. *Hundun*'s kindness and goodness (*shan*, 善) result from the fact that he does not have any openings; that is, he has no organ for distinguishing and judging. As the emperor of the middle (*zhong yang zhi di*, 中央之帝), he is in-different and impartial. The 'middle' (*Mitte*) he inhabits is not a numerical or geometrical middle, not a quantitative middle. Rather, it carries the meaning of *mediation* (*Ver-mittlung*). It has a balancing and harmonizing effect. The seven openings, that is, seven organs for making distinctions, destroy his in-difference, that is, his kindness and goodness.

For the Chinese, the sea is not a symbol of chaos or the abyss, nor is it a mysterious place that lures adventurers. It is neither the sea of Odysseus nor that of Kant and Hegel. It is a place of in-difference, of the unbounded and inexhaustible. In the Far East, the transition from land to sea is not experienced as a transition from a firm ground to an unstable support. It is a transition from the limited to the inexhaustible and comprehensive, from difference to in-difference, from fullness to emptiness, from presencing to absencing, from holding fast to releasement (Gelassenheit). This is true not only of Daoism but also of Zen Buddhism. The moment of *satori* (illumination) is one of a great transition that leads to an oceanic feeling.

With one blow the vast sky suddenly breaks into pieces.
Holy, worldly, both vanished without a trace. . . .
The bright moon shines and the wind rustles in front of the temple.
All waters of all rivers flow into the great sea.[32]

For the Chinese, water, or the sea, is the symbol for a thinking or behaviour that, from moment to moment, adapts and snuggles up to the transforming world and changing things. The world is *not abysmal*. It is merely *manifold* in its manifestations. It is not a *being* but a *path* that permanently changes course. Far Eastern thinking does not circle around identity. Transformations and change are not felt to be a threat. They just represent the natural course of things, to which one needs to adapt. This is a thinking in constellations that are impossible to subsume under a principle of identity. It does not use unchanging coordinates as points of orientation. Rather, its task is to recognize each constellation in good time and to react appropriately to it. As opposed to this re-active and re-acting thinking, Western thinking is active and acting: it tackles the world from a fixed standpoint, even *sets sail to conquer it*.[33] The Chinese sages do not *tackle* or *conquer* the world like those adventurous seafarers; they snuggle up to it. Thinking has to stay as supple as possible, so that it opens itself up to the manifold possibilities that exist. Far Eastern thinking is friendly, in the sense that it does not insist on set axioms and principles. And its wisdom is slow. Because of the absence of fixed rules, hesitation is part of its nature. Wisdom is a *hesitant knowledge*. Slowness and friendliness are the pace of Far Eastern thinking. From this perspective, even Nietzsche was not a thinker friendly towards slowness. In one of his fragments he writes: 'Women react slower than men, the Chinese slower than the Europeans.'[34]

For all his radical revisions, and despite his reversal of Greek metaphysical thinking, Nietzsche remained a Western thinker, that is, an Odysseus figure. His numerous sea and seafaring metaphors betray the Greek origins of his thinking. Heroism and activism dominate his relationship with the sea:

> All speech runs too slowly for me: – I leap into your char-iot, storm! And I shall whip even you with the whip of my malice!
> Like a shout and a jubilation I want to journey over broad seas until I find the blessed isles where my friends dwell – [35]

Nietzsche is driven towards the sea by a longing, an untame-able urge for the unknown, for the mysterious: 'If ever that joy of searching is in me that drives sails toward the undis-covered, if a seafarer's joy is in my joy. . .'.[36] Thinking, for Nietzsche, remains a matter of conquering the sea, setting sail for the unknown:

> Have you never seen a sail go over the sea, rounded and bil-lowed and trembling with the vehemence of the wind?
> Like the sail, trembling with the vehemence of the spirit, my wisdom goes over the sea – my wild wisdom![37]

Appropriation and taking possession continue to determine the relationship towards the world:

> if the world is like a dark jungle and a pleasure garden for all wild hunters, to me it seems even more, and preferably, an abysmal rich sea,

70

– a sea full of colorful fishes and crabs, for whose sake even gods would crave to become fishermen and net casters: so rich is the world in odd things great and small![38]

Nietzsche repeatedly mentions a 'great longing'.[39] 'Longing' is alien to the Far East, which does not know of a radical *somewhere else* for which one could set sail. In this world without mystery, amid the obviousness of the heaven and the self-evident *being-so*, there is no longing, no desire for adventure. Far Eastern culture is not a culture of passion and longing. Its thinking is therefore turned towards the *everyday* in a particular sense: the here and now.

The appearance of water must have reminded Confucius of the fact that there is no stable order, no lasting condition, under the sun: 'Standing on the bank of a river, the Master said, "Look at how it flows on like this, never stopping day or night!"'[40] (*bu she zhou ye*, 不舍晝夜). *She* (舍) also means 'house' and 'dwelling'. Water *does not dwell*. It is *ab-sencing*, as Confucius might have taught. He does not take unchanging, general axioms and principles as points of orientation. Rather, he adapts to the form of each situation as it arises. For this reason, his way of speaking is without stiffness. On one occasion, he tells his pupils: 'There is nothing for me that is absolutely possible or absolutely impossible' (*wu ke wu bu ke*, 無可無不可).[41] Confucius also does not think that there is anything that is absolutely necessary (*wu bi*, 毋必).[42] He avoids everything definitive. For this reason, he does not hold firm opinions (*wu yi*, 毋意). He does not cling on to anything (*wu gu*, 毋固). Confucius never offers a definition. Definitions are a method that leads from the particular to the general. But Confucius's speech does not involve argumentative development. Instead of leading to some place, it always seems to point to the *way*. Despite their brevity, his remarks are not aphoristic. Aphorisms have a certain intellectual pointedness.

71

Confucius's words, by contrast, are round, so to speak; they cannot be sharpened and made to point.

In the last chapter of the *Critique of Practical Reason*, Kant characterizes science as the doctrine of wisdom: 'science (critically sought and methodically directed) is the narrow gate that leads to the *doctrine of wisdom*'.[43] Philosophy, according to Kant, is the guardian of this strict science. However, lacking mathematics as a tool for this task, the philosopher adopts 'a procedure similar to that of *chemistry* – the *separation* . . . of the empirical from the rational', thus isolating something constant, a general law or principle.[44] Thinking should use separation and distinction in order to reach a stable level. In this respect, there is no essential difference between Kant's chemist, with his art of separation, and the Cartesian geologist, who digs down to find a stable, even unshakeable, foundation. In his *Discourse on Method*, Descartes says: 'my whole aim was to reach certainty – to cast aside the loose earth and sand so as to come upon rock or clay'.[45] Descartes' God is nothing but the guardian or guarantor of a certainty that is conceived of as immutable: 'For we understand that God's perfection involves not only his being immutable in himself, but also his operating in a manner that is always utterly constant and immutable.'[46] Thinking attempts to dry out the world's swamp, to give it solid contours, to press it into fixed forms. It is an attempt at *terrestrializing* or *territorializing* thinking, which is the equivalent of *theologizing* it. Far Eastern thinking, by contrast, follows the impulse to let thinking settle beyond fixed forms; it *de-territorializes* and *de-terrestrializes* it, even *oceanizes* it.

Far Eastern cuisine is a de-territorialized way of cooking. Everything is chopped up into small parts. The most diverse ingredients, vegetables, mushrooms, poultry and fish, are put together in inventive, colourful combinations. Hardly anything that is solid or massive, that would need to be *segmented*

72

with a sharp knife, makes it onto the plate. The process of eating is not a *stabbing* with a fork but a *surrounding* with chopsticks. In addition, Far Eastern cuisine has no centre. It falls apart into fragments or parallel events, so to speak. It is also de-territorialized in the sense that the hand and eyes, instead of being fixed on one's own plate, move from plate to plate: the many delicacies belong to everyone, or rather no one. Far Eastern cuisine thus also has a de-subjectivizing or de-individualizing effect. In Western cooking, by contrast, all processes and utensils serve to territorialize and individualize the intake of food.

Kant was a thinker of fear. He must have been haunted by an abysmal fear. Fear even crept up on the old Kant when he was served a thin soup. His complaint was that it had too much sea and not enough solid land. Looking at a pudding dish, he even exclaimed: 'I demand shape, a determined shape.' The old Kant also panicked and despaired when a chair or a pair of scissors on his desk were moved out of position. The old Kant, apparently, had lost all trust in the world. He could at least have set sail and conquered soup. How would he have coped with the sight of that clear Japanese soup whose emptiness and nothingness Roland Barthes describes so deliciously?

> The lightness of the bouillon, fluid as water, the soybean dust or minced green beans drifting within it, the rarity of the two or three solids (shreds of what appears to be grass, filaments of vegetable, fragments of fish) which divide as they float in this little quantity of water give the idea of a clear density, of a nutrivity without grease, of an elixir all the more comforting in that it is pure: something aquatic (rather than aqueous), something delicately marine suggests a spring, a profound vitality.[47]

73

Doing and Happening –
Beyond Active and Passive

> There is no such thing as silence.
> Something is always happening that makes a sound.
> No one can have an idea once he starts really listening.[1]
> John Cage, *Silence: Lectures and Writings*

Some expressions that are very common in the West are
hardly used in Far Eastern languages. In Korea, for instance,
you do not say: 'I think that . . .'. This formulation is grammatically possible, but it would sound very unusual. Instead
you say 'seng-gak-i-dunda', a turn of phrase that is impossible
to translate into English. A rough approximation would be:
'the thought has established itself in me'. Strictly speaking,
however, this translation is wrong because the reflexive pronoun 'itself' subjectifies the thought. The Korean expression
lacks all subjectivity. Rendering it as 'the thought occurred
to me' would be just as wrong. This formulation does not
have a reflexive pronoun, but the verb 'occurred' again suggests something subject-like, and the object 'to me' implies

a receiving, passive subject. The Korean turn of phrase, by contrast, lacks any reference to an addressee. Equally problematic would be 'the thought came to me'. Both the object 'to me' and the verb 'came' press the Korean turn of phrase, which is characterized by a subject-less expanse, back into the narrowness of a subject-based structure. The Korean phrase also lacks the movement of the 'coming thought'. The thought is somehow there, without me doing anything for it. It lies there without imposing itself on me or anybody else. Nor is there a passive subject that suffers something that is happening. What is put into words is a simply lying there; *no one* is really *involved*.

In Korean, a thought is rarely emphasized or marked as being my *own*. In a certain sense, the speaker is completely absent. The speaker retreats into a permanent *it-seems-that*, which is not, however, a relativization of truth. This *it-seems-that* avoids all unconditionality, all finality. It is an absolute semblance insofar as no one can transform it into an unambiguous *this-is-how-it-is* of truth. Truth gives way to an *it-seems-so*. The retreat into the *it seems-so* is also a matter of politeness. Truth is *impolite*. It comes straight along, without taking any detours. It announces itself without any hesitation.

When you say, in English, 'I am looking at the sea', there is nothing unusual about it. In Korean, it sounds very unusual. Instead, one would say 'bada-ga-bo-inda', a turn of phrase that cannot be translated into English. 'The sea is visible' or 'the sea appears to me' are not adequate translations, as the distinction between the seeing subject and the seen object is too clear. The Korean formulation does not explicitly point to a subject *to whom* an object appears. The seeing of the sea is there, is given. 'Looking at', again, has too much directionality about it. The form of perception on which the Korean turn of phrase is based lacks an object as something that is opposed. It is *without direction*. It is a-perspectival. There is

75

no subject taking a position from which an object is *looked at*. The sea is there. At the most, I am the calm resonating space for this 'there'. This turn of phrase opens up a subject-less expanse that completely disappears in the translation 'I am looking at the sea'. The verbs 'dunda' and 'bo-inda' do not express a passive meaning. The Korean language does not distinguish unambiguously between active and passive. In turn, it can very well express happenings in which no subject is involved either as acting or suffering, a happening that simply *takes* place or *comes* about [statt-*findet* oder statt-*hat*]. Such finding and coming would already be too active. In Far Eastern languages, the subject is often left out altogether, so that the verb stands alone, making an unambiguous assignment of an action to a subject impossible. Because of the frequent absence of a subject, the description of an *action* often gives the impression of a sequence of *happenings* or *events* in which no one in particular is involved.

In Old Chinese, too, verbs often are in a state of in-difference between active and passive. To make a passive meaning explicit, passive particles such as *jian* (見, literally 'to see') or *bei* (被, literally 'to suffer') are used. One says, for instance, *jian wu* (見惡, literally 'to see hating') for 'is hated'. A passive does not necessarily have to be marked by a particle. A passive relation can also be deduced from the overall sense of a sentence. Before the Qin dynasty, it was rare for a passive meaning to be expressed by a grammatical particle. A passive relation was indicated simply by mentioning the doer after a preposition, for instance *yu* (於), with the verb expressing nei-ther an active nor a passive relation. An example: *xiao ren yi yu wu* (小人役於物) – the common man is oppressed by worldly things. In the Chinese sentence, the verb *yi* (to oppress) is in the infinitive; it is neither active nor passive.

The English passive construction 'she is loved' expresses something altogether different from the Chinese passive construction, which would literally mean 'she sees loving'. The English passive voice, actually the passive voice of Western languages, reaches deeper. It signifies a constitution, the *state*, a person is in. The expression 'she is loved' permeates the whole body, so to speak, touches every nerve and sinew of a person. Chinese does not have this *depth*, this penetrating energy and determination of *declining*. Flection (literally bending and declining) should be understood physically and psychologically, not just grammatically. It forms, flexes, declines and bends not only the verb but also body and soul. The Chinese 'she sees loving', by contrast, signifies more of a *taking note of a happening*. It does not *decline* the 'soul'.

Japanese also has a form for verbs that is neither passive nor active. In Japanese, a happening that takes place by itself is called *jihatsu*. The reflexive 'by itself' of the English, again, destroys the character of a happening expressed by the Japanese form. There is no subject making *itself* felt in the happening. In English, it is not possible to *evade* the subject. We may therefore call the subject-less happening an 'escaping'. But we could also call it 'absencing'. An essence is, after all, something that asserts *itself* and thereby distinguishes itself from the other. It is a counter-figure to in-difference. Escaping and absencing represent a happening that is simply there without me noticing it, without me intentionally effecting it or allowing it, with me consciously suffering it, that is, a happening beyond subject and object, beyond activity and passivity. Writing, too, is then no longer an act but a subject-less happening. Without my knowledge, without my intention, it happens as if by itself. Yoshida Kenkō's famous book *Essays in Idleness* begins with the following remark: 'What a strange, demented feeling it gives me when I realize I have spent whole days before this inkstone, with nothing better to do, jotting down at random whatever nonsensical thoughts have entered my head.'[2] It is strange because it is an escaping, an absencing. Something happens without my active doing, without my intention, without my will – even without me. Something is there without me having created or suffered it. For this reason, I am astonished about it.

Western culture is not simply a culture of the active mode that is juxtaposed with a Far Eastern culture of a passive mode. Active and passive are siblings. They appear together. The brighter the active becomes, the darker the passive. They are related like light and shadow, like mountain and valley. A pronounced passive mode is possible only in a language and in a culture that possesses a strong emphasis on the active mode, on the determination of a heroically acting subject. If anything, Far Eastern culture is a culture of in-difference between active and passive. In Far Eastern culture, one rarely comes across turns of phrase that are explicitly passive or active, that is, that signify a relation with *acting*. Most expressions retreat into the in-difference of a singular *happening without victim and perpetrator, without guilt and atonement*.

The ancient Greek expression for 'it rains' is 'Huei ho Zeus (or theos)': Zeus or God lets it rain. This divine subject transforms what happens into an act. Apparently, Western thinking finds it hard to conceive of a subject-less happening, a being-so, a simple being-there. The pronoun 'it', as a phantom subject, is an empty reflex of this subjectivizing thinking. In Old Chinese, by contrast, a simple sign – *yu*, meaning 'rain' or 'raining' – stands for 'it rains'.

yu 雨

The sign simply depicts falling raindrops. It does *not* indicate that there is *anyone* who lets it rain. The Chinese draw a few raindrops on paper. The sign *yu* is a very prosaic representation, a simple noticing of a happening, of a being-so that is simply there. All that is to be seen are a few tiny rain-

Illustration 13: Writing as a taking-place

drops. The sign *registers* falling raindrops. It leaves it at that visibility. Rain – *like this* ... *No more*. Such sobriety, such restraint, cannot just be taken for granted. Positing a subject as an *explanation* would be easier. There is no god, no empty subject, to disturb the wonderful stillness of *yu*, this comforting absence. Raining, as something happening, is a simple *like this*. It is flat, so that no subject, no 'demonic' or 'mysterious' it, no god, takes up space there.[3]

> In the summer rain
> > the frogs come right up
> > > to the front door

Daoist thinking, too, aims to take away all character of an action from things. Zhuangzi's famous cook cuts up an ox by moving his knife through the already existing spaces between the joints. As if this effortless cutting already displayed too much activity, Zhuangzi tries to present it as something that is simply happening. Zhuangzi's cook simply sees to it that, *as if all by itself*, 'flop! the whole thing comes apart like a clod of earth crumbling to the ground'[4] (*zhe ran yi jie, ru tu wei di*, 磔然已解 如土委地). It is interesting that *zhe ran* is an onomatopoetic word, imitating the sound of something falling apart. It is a sound that indicates that something is *happening*. It transforms the act of cutting up into a subject-less happening. After the ox has fallen apart, as if by itself, the cook looks around, standing there in self-oblivion (*wei zhi si gu, wei zhi chou chu*, 為之四顧 為之躊躇). He is surprised about what has happened, almost without him doing anything. He seems as astonished as the author of the *Essays on Idleness*.

Interestingly, the Japanese verb form for something happening is also used for the polite form of address (*sonkei*). There is, however, no satisfactory explanation for why something happening without any doing and politeness should belong together. A German sinologist suspects that the nobility of the master consists in the fact that he has servants whom he burdens with the work, in other words, that he lets others do things instead of doing them himself.[5] This is not a convincing explanation. Rather, we must assume that something happening without being intentionally brought about is as such something noble, and that for the Far Eastern sensibility actions, or engaged activity, do not appear noble. For what is noble is to *hold oneself back*, to disappear and to step back behind what is happening without anyone's intention or intervention, without a will being involved and without emphasis on an act. What is noble is *absencing*. Therefore, neither master nor servant is noble. Working, as well as letting others do the work, follows the logic of doing. What is noble is that which rises above any master-slave dialectic. Semantically, the subject is originally both master and slave, both active and passive. The French phrase 'sujet à . . .' means 'being subjected'. One might also say: the subject is a slave who is under the delusion that he is master. What would be noble would be, also from a Buddhist perspective, to escape this delusion of subjectivity. Absencing is a Buddhist ideal, a formula for deliverance. Escaping is deliverance. Doing and clinging on is suffering. Deliverance means escaping from karma, which literally means 'doing' or 'acting'.

One day, Confucius spoke to his disciples thus:

The Master sighed, 'Would that I did not have to speak!'
    Zigong said, 'If the Master did not speak, then how would we little ones receive guidance from you?'
    The Master replied, 'What does Heaven ever say? Yet the four seasons are put in motion by it, and the myriad creatures receive their life from it. What does Heaven ever say?'[6]

Confucius's silence does not aim at the unsayable, the mystery that cannot be captured by language. Confucius does not want to keep silent because language is insufficient and cannot signify its object adequately. It is not a lack but an excess, even a loquaciousness, that discredits language. Confucius's silence is not directed at a transcendence that goes beyond the immanence of language, to which justice can be done only by remaining silent. In any case, the heaven of the Chinese does not stand for a transcendence. It does not have theological depth. Confucius's silence does not contain a centrifugal force that carries it towards the sublime. Confucius does not flee language in favour of a being that escapes language, for which every linguistic expression would be a betrayal, a violation. Confucius's silence is not an *eloquent* silence. Quite the opposite – he wants to avoid all eloquence.

The unsayable, that which escapes language, is not a theme in Far Eastern thinking. In Western discourse, by contrast, it is very common. Language is renounced in favour of a remainder that can be expressed only in song: this would be Celan's or Heidegger's way of proceeding. Only silence can do justice to this divine residue, which is of a metaphysical, aesthetic or – as in Levinas's case – ethical character. On Levinas's 'other', which eludes all discourse, Derrida remarks: 'if one remains within Levinas's intentions, what would a language without phrase, a language which would say nothing, offer to the other? . . . A master who forbids himself the phrase would give nothing. He would have no disciples but only slaves.'[7] Confucius's disciples are not slaves. By keeping silent, he nevertheless makes them think. Zen masters, as is well known, are also taciturn. It is not rare for a master's disciples to achieve *satori* because the master consistently refuses to say anything. Zen masters like to draw on only a few – often meaningless – words. Their silence, however, is *empty*. It does not *refer* to anything. The limited use of language in Zen Buddhism

82

is not an expression of a rejection of language in favour of some unsayable, mysterious essential entity. Language is renounced not because of a 'not enough' but because of a 'too much'. Speaking already presupposes a distance from what is happening. It turns escaping [Entkommnis] into an *occurrence* [Vorkommnis] and departs from the immediacy of what is happening. 'Heaven never speaks' does not mean that, being unfathomable or a riddle, it retreats into mysterious silence. Heaven does not say anything, one might say, because it does not need to say anything. The Western, or Christian, heaven, by contrast, is *eloquent*. The Chinese heaven is neither eloquent nor mute. It is the *simplicity of its 'so'* that makes language completely superfluous. Far Eastern culture is not a culture of the secret or the mystery; it is a culture of *being-so*. Far Eastern thinking is *flat* in a particular sense. It does not immerse itself in the unspeakable. Neither thinking nor the soul has a subterranean vault; there are no murky depths to be dealt with by metaphysics or psychoanalysis.

Confucius remains silent. But he does not remain silent about something. His silence, too, is *empty*. And by keeping silent, he holds *himself* back in absence. This constitutes his friendliness. Usually, silence is unfriendly because it is negative. Confucius's silence, however, is without negativity. Peter Handke writes: 'Isn't consciousness in need of my silence? Does it not flourish only with my kind silence? "He kept silent with kindness": a wonderful phrase! Friendly silence, until it fills the world: ideal.' One might also say: I keep silent with kindness, until I am completely filled by the world. Confucius keeps silent with kindness. Friendly silence is a state of absence and escape. You silence *yourself* away and become *world*. Keeping silent, Confucius becomes *heaven*. This keeping silent is unbounding; it suspends the difference between I and world, active and passive, subject and object. This in-difference constitutes its friendliness.

83

I am part of what is happening, without, however, my *taking* part or *having* a part. Without taking-part and having-a-part, outside taking and having, I *am* yet a part. I am part of the sea's visibility. The sea appears through me. Instead of taking-part and having-a-part, one should better speak of a co-part [Mit-Teil]. I am a co-part of what is happening. Within what is happening, it is impossible to determine *who inhabits the centre and who the periphery*, who is *master* and who *slave* in what is happening. Such happening does not permit a central perspective. No one occupies a position from which what is happening can be looked at in its entirety. Every element of what is happening is a co-part with equal rights. Thus, every co-part can be the centre. The relaxation I feel whenever I say, in Korean, 'bada-ga-bo-inda' – a calmness that completely disappears with the English 'I am looking at the sea' – is probably the result of this absence of an I that would be the source of everything, the result of *no one-ness*.

For Asian aesthetic sensibility, something that happens without a subject being involved, without the imprint of a doing, is both noble and beautiful. The imprint of a subjective act is a typically Western motif. In his *Philosophy of Spirit* (1805/6), Hegel says:

> The human being is this Night . . . here a bloody head suddenly shoots up and there another white shape, only to disappear as suddenly. We see this Night when we look a human being in the eye, looking into a Night which turns terrifying. [For from his eyes] the night of the world hangs out toward us . . . the power to draw images out of this Night or let them fall away: self-positing, internal consciousness, activity.[8]

It is the power that turns night into day, darkness into brightness, chaos into image, into form. It points towards the

84

actionism of a heroic self that posits *itself*, realizes *itself* by *doing*. Nietzsche also found it hard to think beyond doing. But at least he tried to think doing without a doer:

> there is no 'being' behind the deed . . . the 'doer' is invented as an afterthought, – the doing is everything . . . The scientists do no better when they say 'force moves, force causes' and such like, – all our science, in spite of its coolness and freedom from emotion, still stands exposed to the seduction of language and has not rid itself of the changelings foisted upon it, the 'subjects'.[9]

Despite his far-sightedness, Nietzsche was not able to turn from the philosophy of doing and power to the philosophy of happening. This is why he remained a Western thinker. Escaping or absencing are ultimately wholly alien to Nietzsche. With his philosophy of power and will, he remains more or less attached to subjectivity.

The world is a *verb*, or, to be more precise, an infinitive, a happening that is in many respects infinite, that is, undetermined. In positive terms, it points to an endless process of transformation. Chinese verbs are also undetermined with respect to person, time and number. They simply do not conjugate. Neither Chinese thinking nor the Chinese language knows the finality of a *finitum*. Depending on its position, a Chinese sign can be used as a noun, adjective, verb or preposition. A sign can oscillate between verb and preposition. In Far Eastern languages, an adjective has a special status. It is often used like a verb. It could be put like this: an adjective is not a property of a noun, not an accident of a substance to which it belongs. Rather, it is a certain state that pertains to what is happening overall – to the verb. Another way of putting it would be to say that nouns, adjectives and adverbs are *co-parts* of something that is happening, that is, of

85

a verb. Thus, a verb in its infinitive form can stand all by its own, without any further determination. It is very comforting to look upon a verb in this infinite, even innocent, state. It knows of neither an active nor a passive compulsion, neither action nor passion, neither guilt nor atonement, neither doer nor victim. The brilliance of some haikus also rests on such happening without doing:

On a duck's wing
    the soft snow mounts and mounts;
        ah, this calmness
            Shiki

a spring unseen:
    on the back of a mirror,
        plum blossoms
           Bashō[10]

To succumb unconsciously and without desire to the pleasant smell of absence, to be absent, someone absent, without I, to immerse *oneself* in the landscape of emptiness, to be simply its co-part – that is probably the ideal of quite a number of Far Eastern poets.

問余何意栖碧山
笑而不答心自閑
桃花流水杳然去
別有天地非人間

You ask why I've settled in these emerald mountains,
and so I smile, mind at ease of itself, and say nothing.

Peach blossoms drift streamwater away deep in mystery:
it's another heaven and earth, nowhere among people.
           Li Po[11]

Illustration 14: Landscape of emptiness

Heidegger may have repeatedly allowed himself to be touched by Far Eastern thinking, but in many respects he remained a Western thinker, a philosopher of essence. His silence is also *eloquent*. It is *on the way* towards the 'hidden', the 'origin', that escapes the word. As Heidegger says, truth must be achieved 'by silence' [er-schweigen].[12] A famous passage of Heidegger's in *On the Way to Language* runs: 'An "is" arises where the word breaks up. To break up here means that the sounding word returns into soundlessness, back to whence it was granted: into the ringing of stillness.'[13] Heidegger also frequently uses the trope of the 'way', but his 'way' differs from the way as *dao*. 'Holzwege' are paths in the forest that come to an 'abrupt stop where the wood is untrodden'.[14] They immerse themselves 'in the inaccessible self-sheltering / locality'.[15] The way of Daoism does not know of such *abruptness* or *depth*. It does not retreat to the 'untrodden' or 'inaccessible'. *Dao* is a way of walking. It escapes determination only because it constantly shifts direction. The dialectic of darkness and light, hiddenness and revealing, revelation and withdrawal[16] is not the fundamental trait of the *dao*.

Heidegger is not a philosopher of the *way*. He circles *being*. He associates being with stillness, silence and duration. Process and transformation, which characterize the *dao*, are not traits of being:

'To while' [Weilen] means: 'to tarry', 'to remain still', 'to pause and keep to oneself', namely in rest. In a beautiful verse Goethe says:

The fiddle stops and the dancer whiles.

'Whiling', 'tarrying', 'perpetuating' is indeed the old sense of the word 'being' [sein].[17]

Heidegger's being, which retreats into hiddenness, does not capture the immanence of *being-so* that dominates Far Eastern thinking. *Being-so* is flatter and more everyday than Heidegger's 'being'.

> Yesterday, today, it is just as it is. In the sky the sun rises and the moon wanes. In front of the window, the mountain rises high and the deep river flows.[18]

In *The Principle of Reason*, Heidegger quotes Angelus Silesius: 'A heart that is calm in its ground, God-still, as he will, / Would gladly be touched by him: it is his lute-play.'[19] Without God, without a divine player, the heart remains without music. In another place, Heidegger gives an idiosyncratic twist to Leibniz's 'Cum Deus calculate fit mundus' (When God calculates, world comes to be), suggesting it might better be rendered as: 'When God plays, world comes to be.'[20] God plays. The music he plays is the world. In the end, there is not so much difference between the calculating and the playing God. Even a playing God has too much of *doing*, of subjectivity, about him. He is not *absencing*. Zhuangzi's lute is not the lute of God. It has a peculiar property. It sounds only once the player *exits*, when no one is *present*. Without any player, without any *virtuosity* of a divine or human subject, without ever being touched by anyone, it radiates sounds of unheard beauty and enticing fragrances of absence.

Greeting and Bowing – Friendliness

I lifted my hand, as a greeting to the bird in the bush, and
felt the form of the one thus greeted in the palm of my
hand.[1]

Peter Handke, *Phantasien der Wiederholung*

The word 'Grüßen' (Old High German: *gruozen* [to greet])
has an interesting etymology. It originally was anything but
friendly, meaning 'cause to speak', 'provoke', 'unsettle' or
'attack'.[2] *Gruozen* is related to Gothic 'gretan', which means
'to shout' or 'to make weep'. *Gruozen*, interestingly, is an
onomatopoeia. It sounds very coarse and guttural. There is
probably a close etymological connection between *gruozen* and
'Groll' [grudge], which is also an onomatopoeia.[3] Originally,
to greet someone must have involved emitting a dark, guttural, threatening sound. *Gruozen* is also strikingly similar to
another onomatopoeia, the Old High German *grunnezzen*
(ninth century: *grunnizon*), meaning 'to grumble' or 'to bear
a grudge'. *Grunnezzig* means 'grim' or 'grumbling'.[4] In New

High German, *grunnezzen* means 'to grunt'. These acoustic similarities suggest that a genealogy of 'greeting' would not lead us to a *noble* origin.

Initially, the *other* represents a possible threat and danger to my existence. The other has an unsettling effect. The guttural sound of *gruozen* is probably an immediate reaction to the *primordial threat* posed by the other, another *human being*. By emitting a guttural, threatening sound I challenge the other to fight. I *gruoze* him. The unsettling effect of the other disappears completely only once he has given up his opposition by fully submitting to me. The archaic scene in Hegel's *Philosophy of Spirit* in which two primitive human beings meet for the first time, the scene between master and slave, is a scene of *gruozen*. It begins with an aggressive, challenging *gruozen*. Hegel writes: '*They must . . . hurt each other; that each of them posits himself in his individual existence as an excluding totality must become real; the insult is necessary.*'⁵ The first word is not a friendly one. By uttering a threatening sound, each announces his entitlement to the *totality*. Thus, a fight is unavoidable. The one who, fearing his death, bows to the other becomes the slave. The one who fearlessly prefers death to submission becomes the master. The master does not greet his slave in a friendly way. Rather, he has to subject him to a latent and permanent threat so that the slave remains a slave. The one who gains power, *mastery [Herrschaft]*, extends *his own existence* in the other. For him, the other does not exist. The other does not assert *himself*. All he does is carry out the master's will. He is *the master's* slave. He is only an extension of the master. Thus, the master's existence stretches into the other. Power restores the master's freedom, which was briefly in question when he faced the other. Despite the other, he *remains*, even *dwells*, freely *within himself*.

Greeting has a particular genealogy. It was preceded by a fight, a challenging *gruozen*, which must have sounded similar to *grunnizon*. The genealogy of greeting points back to the scene of injury and fighting, of submission and domination. *Gruozen* is the primordial sound of fear, terror and defence. Hegel's master-slave dialectic ends in mutual recognition. It describes the interpersonal drama that leads from fighting to the subjugation of the other, and then to mutual recognition, at which point it even *relaxes* into a friendly greeting. Only with mutual recognition does the guttural *gruozen* turn into a greeting, which, although it may not yet be a soothing sound, at least tells the other that he is not unsettling me, that I recognize him and shall accept him as an other.

Greeting resolves, through *dialogue*, the interpersonal tension that leads to fighting and subjugation. The dialectic that defuses the challenging *gruozen*, turning it into a greeting, is a process of dialogical mediation. A dialogue is a binary relation between *persons*. The antagonistic tension is not resolved by a negation of the other. Greeting, after all, rests on an other. The dialogical mediation that leads to reconciliation, to recognition, takes the antagonistic sharpness out of the relation between counterparts.

Heidegger, too, conceives of greeting from the perspective of dialogical recognition. In his lecture on Hölderlin's *Remembrance*, there is a short passage in which Heidegger turns to the phenomenon of greeting. A 'genuine greeting', Heidegger says, 'is an address [Zuspruch] that grants to that which is greeted the essential rank due to it, and thus comes to acknowledge the greeted from out of the nobility of its essence, through this acknowledgment letting it be what it is'.[6] The friendliness of greeting consists in this letting be, in this *releasement* [Gelassenheit] of the other. Greeting is first of all an event of *essencing* [Wesen]: 'That which is due beforehand to any being is the essence from out of which it is what it is.'[7] The dialogue of mutual greeting presents an image of the essence of the *persons* involved. It is a *dia-legein*.

92

To greet one another means to help one another to realize one's essence. Greeting is a process of recognition. To greet an other means to recognize him in his essence, that is, in what he *is*, his person. The one who is greeted is afforded his essence, his person; it is even greeted to him [zugegrüßt]. A greeting, one might say, means that the one who is greeted is properly *presencing* [lässt den Gegrüßten eigens anwesen]. A greeting is a process of distinguishing insofar as the two who are greeting each other separate themselves into their own proper essences. A greeting therefore does not create the nearness of a fusion. Rather, the greeter greets the other one in the distance, in the otherness of the other's essence:

> In the genuine greeting there even lies concealed that mysterious stringency whereby, each time, those greeting one another are on each occasion directed into the remoteness of their own essence and its preservation; for everything essential is, by virtue of what is its own, in each case unconditionally remote from what is other.[8]

A dialogue does not aim at fusion. It always takes place in an *in between* that separates *and* mediates. Fusion makes this dialogical *in between* disappear. A 'genuine greeting' always retains the 'remoteness' that is inscribed in the *in between*. The in between guarantees the dialogical *to and fro*, that is, the 'transition' *between* the separate essences who inhabit the in between as *persons*: 'Yet it is this remoteness alone that also ensures the moments of transition from one to the other. Genuine greeting is one way of such transition.'[9] The remoteness, the in between, disappears not only in the case of a fusion but also in the case of a one-sided appropriation of the other. Heidegger's 'genuine greeting' is a *friendly* greeting insofar as it *lets* the other *be* in the remoteness or otherness of his essence, insofar as it does not seize the other. Dialogical friendliness consists precisely in this renunciation: 'The act of greeting is a reaching out to that which is greeted, a touching . . . that yet does not touch, a grasping that yet never needs to "grip" because it is at the same time a letting go.'[10] *Friendliness is releasement.*

The one who *gruozt* challenges the other to a fight; he wants to posit himself as an excluding totality. He demands *everything* for *himself.* The other has to be *nothing.* That is why this totality is excluding. In this totality, the other has a place only as a slave who carries out my will, who extends my own existence. Heidegger's 'genuine greeting' represents a complete reversal of this challenging *gruozen.* A genealogy is often the history of a reversal. Heidegger is not fully aware of this dialectic, this long history of recognition, which leads from archaic hostility to the friendliness of dialogical greeting. He thinks neither in dialectical nor in genealogical terms. The 'genuine', which is genealogically later, derived, and mediated, is taken as the 'origin'.[11] The 'genuine greeting' has come a long way from its genealogical origin. As opposed to the original *gruozen*, where someone tries to take possession of everything for himself, the one who greets in a friendly way 'want[s] nothing for himself'. He cares only about the other. He grants the one he greets what is due to the other, that is, his essence:

> To the extent that the one greeting necessarily tells of himself at all and in a certain respect, he says precisely that he wants nothing for himself, but rather turns everything toward that which is greeted, namely, all of that which is promised to that which is greeted in such greeting. This means all that is due to that which is greeted, as that which it is.[12]

The friendliness of greeting is based on the dialogical nature of recognition, of decidedly letting-be, of permitting

94

the presencing of the other. The space in which greeting takes place becomes charged with a dialogical tension, condenses into a dialogical *interior space*. The dialogical space is *full*, so to speak. It is filled with *essence*. A jostling inwardness emerges, a jostling of *gazes*, a jostling of persons, a jostling of words. In a dialogue, the participants prompt each other to proper *presencing*, to fill the room with one's presence. Proper *presencing* is, after all, the precondition for any dialogue.

The demand to *stand-opposite-the-other* as a proper *I*, to stand upright as a person, is inherent to greeting. It finds expression in particular in the *gaze*. The greeting returns the *gaze of the other*. It would be only a mild exaggeration to say that Far Eastern culture is a *culture without gaze*. The gaze is *the other*. In Japan it is considered impolite to look the other straight in the eye. The lack of the gaze is the reason why, when one finds oneself among the jostling crowds that are so characteristic of Far Eastern cities, one does not feel beset. The lack of gaze fills the crowded cities with a particular emptiness and absence.

Greeting is *erecting*. Its composure is a *standing* opposite. Standing, steadfastness, the independent standing for oneself when meeting the other, or withstanding or recognizing him – these are all fundamental traits of *essencing*. The Japanese bow is a counter-movement to this. The person is bowed into an absence. It is not a dialogical event, as is clear from the fact that those who are greeting do not look each other in the eyes. Bowing allows the gaze to disappear. Dialogical space is opened up only by the mutual gaze. At the moment of bowing, you look *nowhere*. This nowhere marks the nothing, the emptiness, the in-difference in which the gaze is submersed.

In a deep bow, the body posture is the opposite of standing opposite, the dialogical posture. Those who bow form a flat plane together, *levelling*, so to speak, the difference between the people standing opposite each other. This plane levels the *standing self* into an *absence*. Often, the plane made up of the two who are bowing does not form a *straight* line. It is not a case of bowing *to* the other, in direct *opposition* to him. Rather, the extended lines of the deeply bowing bodies cross over. This crossing over is the final definite suspension of person-like opposition. You do not bow *to* the other but *into* emptiness.

Who is greeting whom? *No one is greeting.* No one is greeting no one. The deep bow levels the person into a no one. Roland Barthes, in his book on Japan, *Empire of Signs*, also asks the question '*Who is saluting whom?*' and answers: 'The salutation here can be withdrawn from any humiliation or any vanity, because it literally salutes *no one*' (*il ne salue personne*).[13] A Japanese bow does not have a *person* opposite itself. Because there is no person opposite, there is also no subjugation. It is the Western mythology of the 'person' that makes the deep bow seem like a submissive act. A Western observer must be irritated by the fact that the submission takes place on both sides. Who subjugates whom? Who submits to whom? The mutual subjugation suspends the relation of subjugation.

Unlike those involved in a dialogical greeting, those who bow do not retreat 'into the remoteness of their own essence and its preservation'. Rather, they remove *themselves* into absence. By bowing deeply, one negates *oneself*. In bowing, one steps back into absence. Instead of a mutual *presencing*, of helping each other into each other's essences, the aim is *absencing*. The spatiality of deep bowing is not one of *nearness*. Nearness keeps those involved at a distance from each other. They do not draw nearer. Nor does the suspension of self lead to a fusion with the other. Deep bowing maintains an *in between*. This in between, however, is neither *inter* nor *dia*. It is neither interpersonally nor dialogically *charged*. This *in between*, rather, is *empty*. The absencing gaze removes the

Illustration 15: No one is greeting

dialogical, empties the space of deep bowing, making this space an *empty* in-between.

The *grammar of bowing* has no *nominative* or *accusative*, neither a subjugating *subject* nor a subjugated *object*, neither *active* nor *passive*. It has no *declination* [Beugung]. The mutual bowing suspends the different *cases*. This *absence of cases* constitutes its *friendliness*. Deep bowing does not decline the nominative, which would be the case corresponding to the uprightly standing I, into an accusative. Levinas's ethics of the other, which distances itself from the ethics of freedom as well as the ethics of dialogue, tries to leave behind for good the I 'set up in the nominative in its identity'. But in doing so, it uses a violent *declination*. The nominative is declined into the 'accusative': 'Not strictly speaking an ego set up in the nominative in its identity, but first constrained to . . . It is set up as it were in the accusative form, from the first responsible

97

Illustration 16: To whom is the bowing addressed?

and not being able to slip away.'[14] The other declines – bends – me into a 'hostage'. Without this violent declination, the I would straighten up again into an unbendable nominative. The ethics of friendliness leaves behind not only the nominative but also the accusative – in fact, the idea of cases as such. It also leaves the dialogical interior space and moves into the space of absencing, into the empty in between that is *occupied* neither by the I nor by the other.

Deep bowing is based on the decision to defuse the precarious situation of the person opposite not by dialogic means but instead by levelling it into an in-difference. A deep bow does not mediate between *persons*, does not reconcile anyone with anyone else. Rather, it empties and de-internalizes those involved into *absencing* individuals. In Japan, bowing certainly follows a subtle code of politeness that also has a social hierarchy inscribed into it. But it contains a structural element that is deeply Buddhist, that would be inconceivable without the Buddhist idea of emptiness. Buddhism is a religion of absencing. Buddhist emptiness (*kong*) empties essence into absencing. It does not know of any 'God' – that would be a superlative form of essence. Essences are distinguishing; they create differences. Absencing, which must be understood as something active, turns difference into in-difference. It *noths* [*nichtet*] difference.[15] Example sixty-eight of the *Bi-yan-lu*[16] expresses this movement of absencing:

> Yangshan (Hui-dji) asked Sansheng (Hui-jan): 'What's your name?' Sansheng said, 'Hui-dji.' Yangshan said, 'But Hui-dji, that's me!' Sansheng said, 'Then my name is Hui-jan.' . . . Yangshan laughed mightily: Ha ha ha![17]

A soothing fragrance of absencing drifts through this genuinely Zen Buddhist scene of in-difference. *I am you.* This, however, is not a statement of identity – if it were, it would still follow the logic of essence – but a statement of absencing. *I am you* because there is no identity, no compulsion towards essence, that *distinguishes* the I from the you. Yangshan's mighty laughter laughs off any difference. In this scene, the transition from the one to the other does not take a dialogical form. Rather, it takes place out of in-difference, out of the empty in between. The return to one's own name – 'I am I' – is pervaded by an absence that affords the 'I am I' a soothing ease and releasement [Gelassenheit]. The I loses all finality and rigidity. Thus, only a moment later the 'I am I' returns effortlessly to 'I am you'. Absencing allows for this released [*gelassen*], friendly transition. The mighty laughter of Yangshan still resounds through the land in which the deep bow has become a religion, the *religion of absencing*.

99

NOTES

Epigraph
1 Walter Benjamin, *Berlin Childhood around 1900*, Cambridge, MA: Harvard University Press, 2006, p. 134.

Preface
1 Elias Canetti, The Secret *Heart of the Clock: Notes, Aphorisms, Fragments 1973–1985*, New York: Farrar, Straus, Giroux, 1989, p. 129.

Essencing and Absencing – Living Nowhere
1 Transl. note: There are several translations of this sentence. I follow the suggestion by Stefan Stenudd on https://www.taois tic.com/fake-laotzu-quotes/fake-laotzu-quote-A_good_travel er.htm. Alternative translations include: 'The good traveller leaves no cart rut', in Laozi, *Daodejing* (chapter 27), Oxford: Oxford University Press, 2008, p. 57.
2 Plato, *Symposium* (211b), in *Complete Works*, Indianapolis: Hackett, 1997, pp. 457–505; here: p. 493.
3 Ibid., p. 486 (203d).
4 Gottfried Wilhelm Leibniz, *The Principles of Philosophy, or,*

Monadology, in *Philosophical Essays*, Indianapolis: Hackett, 1989, pp. 213–25.

5 Ibid., § 7, p. 214.
6 Ibid., § 15, p. 215.
7 Ibid., § 63, p. 221.
8 Ibid., § 56, p. 220.
9 Ibid., § 7, p. 210.
10 Gottfried Wilhelm Leibniz, *Die philosophischen Schriften*, Vol. 7, Berlin: Weidmann, 1890, p. 289. [The English translation follows Martin Heidegger, *The End of Philosophy*, Chicago: University of Chicago Press, 2003, p. 50.]
11 Martin Heidegger, 'The Origin of the Work of Art', in *Off the Beaten Track*, Cambridge: Cambridge University Press, 2002, p. 26.
12 Martin Heidegger, 'Ansprache zum 80. Geburtstag Ludwig von Fickers', in *Gesamtausgabe*, Vol. 16, Frankfurt am Main: Klostermann, 2000, pp. 563–4; here: p. 563.
13 Zhuangzi, *The Complete Works of Zhuangzi*, New York: Columbia University Press, 2013, p. 57.
14 As well as meaning 'simple', the Chinese sign 'dan' can mean 'non-desiring' or 'indifferent'. It could thus also be translated as 'absent'. Then the translation of '*you xin yu dan* [遊心於淡]' would be 'let the heart wander in absence'. Zhuangzi, *Complete Works*, p. 56.
15 Laozi, *Daodejing*, p. 31: 'She is called "the shape without a shape", "the image of what is not a thing".'
16 Zhuangzi, *Complete Works*, p. 182. 'I go nowhere and don't know how far I've gotten.'
17 Ibid., p. 87.
18 François Jullien mostly excludes Buddhism from his view of China. According to him, Indian thinking, out of which Buddhism developed, is 'metaphysical', and thus follows his controversial claim that it is fundamentally different from Chinese thinking. Buddhist emptiness, 'kong', he holds, is the 'non-existence' that is part of the 'metaphysics' of 'being and non-being', whereas Daoist emptiness, 'xu', is that functional openness that allows the full development of an effect. Jullien's views on Buddhism are surprisingly sweeping and one-sided.

101

His talk about an 'Indo-European' metaphysics in connection with Buddhist emptiness is dubious. The 'philosophy of emptiness' of the Indian philosopher Nagarjuna, who was influenced by Mahayana Buddhism, certainly is anti-metaphysical. It turns any metaphysical assumption into emptiness. As is well known, Buddha himself refused to engage with genuinely metaphysical questions such as those about the creation of the world or the immortality of the soul. In this regard, he resembles Confucius, who is said to have refused to undertake any investigation into what is hidden. Interestingly, Jullien, while keeping Buddhist thinking out of his China, draws on European thinkers such as Plotinus, Augustine and Kant – all of whom were influenced by Christianity – and uses them as the antagonists of his Chinese thinkers. But the origins of Christianity, after all, are not 'Greek' or 'Indo-European'. How, then, are we to understand Europe without Christianity?

19 Dōgen, *Shōbōgenzō zuimonki: Unterweisungen zum wahren Buddha-Weg*, Heidelberg: Werner Kristkeitz, 1997, p. 168. [The English edition does not contain this exact wording. But see e.g. Dōgen, *Shōbōgenzō zuimonki*, Vol. 1, Moraga, CA: BDK, 2007: 'We have already left our families and left our hometowns; we rely on clouds and rely on waters' (pp. 59f.) The annotation to this sentence says: 'In China and Japan monks are commonly referred to as *unsui*, which means "clouds and water"' (p. 63).]

20 Zhuangzi, *Complete Works*, p. 82.

21 Ibid., pp. 182f.

22 Ibid., pp. 56f. [The English translation uses the term 'Nameless Man'.]

23 Ibid., p. 3. [The English edition translates this as 'no self'.]

24 Ibid.

25 See ibid., pp. 65f.: 'The people have their constant inborn nature. To weave for their clothing, to till for their food – that is the Virtue they share.'

26 In section 55 of the *Daodejing*, Laozi uses a rather explicit image to illustrate pure vitality without desire. He talks about the penis (*zu*) being aroused without any knowledge of the difference between the sexes. A direct translation of this image

has often been avoided. Richard Wilhelm, a Christian missionary, translates the passage thus: 'It [i.e. the child] does not yet know anything about man and woman, and yet its blood moves.' (Laozi, *Tao te king: Das Buch vom Sinn und Leben*, Munich: Anaconda, p. 67.) [The edition used here has a straightforward translation: 'He does not yet know the harmony of female and male yet his penis is aroused' (p. 115). It adds the following explanatory note: 'most versions have *yang* and some interpretations read this as the male infant's penis. In the Mawangdui version the character used clearly refers to the male sexual organ. It should be noted that the Chinese term specifically refers to the sexual organ of an infant' (p. 180).]

27 Laozi, *Daodejing*, p. 9: 'The government of the Sage is thus: He empties his mind, fills his belly; / Weakens his will, strengthens his bones.'

28 Ibid., p. 115.

29 Ibid., p. 27.

30 Lin-Chi, *The Teachings of Zen Master Lin-Chi*, Boston: Shambala, 1993, p. 77.

31 Dōgen, *Shōbōgenzō zuimonki*, Vol. 3, Moraga, CA: BDK, 2008, p. 293.

32 Zhuangzi, *Complete Works*, p. 185.

33 Ibid., p. 98. [The German version begins 'Ruhe, Gelassenheit, Abwesenheit, Leere und Nicht-Tun', literally: 'Calmness, serenity, absence, emptiness and inaction'.]

34 Famous examples are the wheel and vessels:

> Thirty spokes held in one hub;
> – In beingless [Nichts] (*wu*, not *xu*) lies the cartwheel's usefulness;
> Moulding clay into pots;
> – In beingless lies the pot's usefulness;
> Chiselling doors and windows to make a room;
> – In beingless lies the room's usefulness;
> Therefore,
> Possess something to make it profit you;
> Take it as nothing to make it useful for you. (Laozi, *Daodejing*, p. 25)

103

35 François Jullien, *Treatise on Efficacy: Between Western and Chinese Thinking*, Honolulu: University of Hawai'i Press, 2004, p. 112.
36 Laozi, *Daodejing*, p. 141.
37 Jullien, *Treatise on Efficacy*, p. 116.
38 Ibid., p. 174.
39 Ibid.
40 Ibid.
41 See Laozi, *Daodejing*, p. 65. Jullien's strong focus on effects and efficacy may itself be of 'European' origin.
42 Zhuangzi, *Complete Works*, p. 59. [The passage following the ellipsis is not part of the English edition.]
43 Ibid., p. 98.
44 Bi-yan-lu, *Meister Yuän-wu's Niederschrift von der Smaragdenen Felswand*, Munich: Hanser, 1964, p. 145. [The passage is not contained in the English edition: *The Blue Cliff Record [Bi-yan-lu]*, compiled by Ch'ung-hsien and commented upon by K'o-ch'in, trans. Thomas Cleary, Berkeley: Numata Center for Buddhist Translation and Research, 1998.] In this context, too, François Jullien tries to keep Buddhism away from Chinese thought. In Zhuangzi, he says, the mirror escapes 'mystical employment and is understood in an entirely different way': 'The virtue of the mirror is that it accepts but does not hold; it reflects everything it encounters but allows things to pass by without clinging to them. It does not reject or retain. It allows things to appear and disappear without clinging to them.' (François Jullien, *Vital Nourishment: Departing from Happiness*, New York: Zone Books, 2007, pp. 117f.) This description of the Daoist mirror is a good characterization of the mirror used in Zen Buddhism to illustrate the 'empty heart' (*wu xin*). Jullien does not explain the sense in which Zen Buddhism is 'mystical', the sense in which it is closer to Western mysticism than to Daoism. Let us remind ourselves of the famous words of the Zen Master Linji, quoted above (see note 30): 'When you get hungry, eat your rice; / when you get sleepy, close your eyes. / Fools may laugh at me, / but wise men will know what I mean.' In other words, the Zen Buddhist sage also takes care of the 'belly', and the 'belly' is probably not an organ of 'mysticism'.

45 Johann Gottlieb Fichte, *The Vocation of Man*, Chicago: The Open Court Publishing Company, 1931, p. 32.

46 Zhuangzi, *Complete Works*, p. 99 and p. 139.

47 Ibid., p. 120.

48 Immanuel Kant, *Anthropology from a Pragmatic Point of View*, Cambridge: Cambridge University Press, 2006, p. 130 (transl. mod.).

49 Ibid.

50 Zhuangzi, *Complete Works*, p. 2.

51 Ibid., p. 45.

52 Laozi, *Daodejing*, p. 71.

53 Ibid., p. 145.

54 Zhuangzi, *Complete Works*, p. 82.

55 Ibid., p. 120.

56 Ibid., p. 18.

57 See Byung-Chul Han, *The Philosophy of Zen Buddhism*, Cambridge: Polity, 2022, Chapter 4: 'Dwelling Nowhere', pp. 58–68.

58 François Jullien may want to keep Buddhism away from his China, but his description of Chinese blandness is deeply Buddhist: 'Its [i.e. blandness's] season is late autumn, when chrysanthemum petals are falling, touched by frost: the last colors of the year are fading, an erasing that happens on its own, in simpler withdrawal.' (François Jullien, *In Praise of Blandness: Proceeding from Chinese Thought and Aesthetics*, New York: Zone Books, 2004, p. 94.) The painful charm of the falling chrysanthemum petals, the grace of disappearance, is not really typical of Daoism. Jullien even uses terms such as 'l'absence' and 'l'abondon', which, according to his image of China, are not 'indigenous' to its culture: 'As usual, it is autumn. The atmosphere, introduced with this evocation of purity . . . swells with the feeling of absence. All tangible signs gesture toward their own relinquishing.' Ibid., p. 114.

59 Like many poets of blandness, Li Bo lived in the time of the Tang Dynasty, during which Buddhism flourished.

60 Transl. note: Translated from the German version in Matsuo Bashō, *Auf schmalen Pfaden durchs Hinterland*, Mainz: Dieterich'sche Verlagsbuchhandlung, 2011, p. 42.

105

61 Zhuangzi, *Complete Works*, p. 132.
62 Ibid., p. 53.
63 All quotations from Kafka's story: Franz Kafka, 'The Cares of a Family Man', in *Collected Stories*, London: Everyman, 1993, pp. 183–5.
64 Leibniz, *The Principles of Philosophy, or, Monadology*, in *Philosophical Essays*, pp. 213–25; here: p. 213.
65 Plato, Symposium, in *Complete Works*, pp. 457–505; here: p. 493 (211b).

Closed and Open – Spaces of Absencing

1 *The Blue Cliff Record*, p. 82.
2 Thinking does not reach a final closure either. An awareness of in-difference is inherent in Far Eastern thinking, which shies away from sharp incisions. Finality and the unconditional are avoided. This thinking strives to achieve a hovering between differences, rather than to let them solidify into dichotomous opposition. The lack of finality makes thinking friendly.
3 Georg Wilhelm Friedrich Hegel, *Aesthetics: Lectures on Fine Art*, Vol. 2, Oxford: Clarendon, 1975, p. 685.
4 Ibid., p. 687.
5 Ibid., p. 685.
6 Ibid., p. 693.
7 Ibid., p. 686.
8 Ibid., p. 690.
9 On his travels through Greece, Martin Heidegger noted: 'Over the steep foot of the mountain stood the gleaming-white ruins of the temple in a strong sea breeze. For the wind these few standing columns were the strings of an invisible lyre, the song of which the far-seeing Delian god let resonate over the Cycladic world of islands.' Martin Heidegger, *Sojourns: The Journey to Greece*, New York: SUNY, 2005, p. 43.
10 Hegel, *Aesthetics: Lectures on Fine Art*, Vol. 2, p. 690 (transl. mod.).
11 Ibid., p. 689.
12 Ibid., p. 686.
13 Ibid., p. 688.

14 See Shin'ichi Hisamatsu, 'Kunst und Kunstwerke im Zen-Buddhismus', in Ryōsuke Ohasi (ed.), *Die Philosophie der Kyōto-Schule*, Freiburg and Munich: Karl Alber, 1990, pp. 222–34. [For an English version, see Shin'ichi Hisamatsu, *Zen and the Fine Arts*, New York: Kodansha International, 1971, pp. 28–38.]

15 Hegel, *Aesthetics: Lectures on Fine Art*, Vol. 2, p. 734.

16 Ibid.

17 Ibid.

18 Ibid., p. 733.

19 Georg Wilhelm Friedrich Hegel, *Aesthetics: Lectures on Fine Art*, Vol. 1, Oxford: Clarendon, 1975, p. 520.

20 Walter Benjamin, 'Surrealism', in *Selected Writings*, Vol. 2, Part 1 (1927–1930), Cambridge, MA: Harvard University Press, 1999, pp. 207–21; here: p. 209.

Light and Shadow – The Aesthetics of Absencing

1 Immanuel Kant, *Critique of Judgment*, Indianapolis: Hackett, 1987, p. 166.

2 Yoshida Kenkō, *The Miscellany of a Japanese Priest: Being a Translation of Tsure-Zure Gusa*, London: Humphrey Milford, 1914, pp. 105f. [The German title of this book would literally translate as 'Observations out of Stillness'.]

3 Tanizaki Junichiro, *In Praise of Shadows*, London: Vintage, 2019, p. 19.

4 Shōji is the Japanese name for the sliding paper doors that are common across the Far East.

5 Ibid., p. 30.

6 Ibid., p. 34.

7 Ibid.

8 Ibid., p. 26.

9 Dōgen, *Shōbōgenzō*, Vol. 1, p. 218.

Knowledge and Daftness – On the Way to Paradise

1 Matsuo Bashō, *Bashō's Haiku: Selected Poems by Matsuo Bashō*, New York: SUNY, 2004, p. 112.

2 Heinrich von Kleist, 'On the Marionette Theatre', in *The Drama Review: TDR*, Vol. 16, No. 3, The 'Puppet' Issue (Sept. 1972), pp. 22–6; here: p. 23 (transl. mod.).

3 Ibid., p. 24.
4 Ibid., p. 22 and p. 24.
5 Ibid., p. 22.
6 Ibid. (transl. mod.).
7 Ibid.
8 Georg Wilhelm Friedrich Hegel, 'Travel Diary through the Bernese Alps (1796)', in Sean Ireton and Caroline Schaumann (eds.), *Mountains and the German Mind: Translations from Gessner to Messner (1541–2009)*, Woodbridge: Boydell & Brewer, 2020, pp. 99–119; here: p. 112.
9 Ibid., p. 104, (transl. amended).
10 Ibid. (transl. mod.).
11 Kleist, 'On the Marionette Theatre', p. 24.
12 Ibid.
13 Ibid., 26.
14 Plato, *Phaedrus*, in *Collected Works*, pp. 506–56; here: p. 525 (246d).
15 See 'The Man Who Lost His Memory', in *Lieh-Tzu: A Taoist Guide to Practical Living*, Boston: Shambala, 1995, pp. 97–8.
16 Zhuangzi, *Complete Works*, pp. 152f. [In the English edition, a footnote explains the expression 'matching up "Heaven with "Heaven"' as follows: 'That is, matching his own innate nature with that of the tree.' A literal translation of the German version would be: 'Because I have thus brought together my nature with the nature of the material, the people think it is a divine work.']
17 Ibid., p. 81 (transl. mod.).
18 Transl. note: my translation.
19 Ibid., p. 200 (transl. mod.).
20 Transl. note: my translation.
21 Laozi, *Daodejing*, p. 135.
22 See Zhuangzi, *Complete Works*, p. 26.
23 See ibid., p. 179. Richard Wilhelm's translation is unfortunate. It says: 'Dominate your body.' Wilhelm frequently speaks of 'domination' where the Chinese does not mention it at all. He for instance translates '*wang de zhi ren*' (王德之人, literally: 'a man of magnificent wisdom and morality') as 'The man who dominates life like a king . . .' (see *Das wahre Buch vom*

südlichen Blütenland, Jena: Eugen Diederichs, 1912, p. 85). In this context, 'wáng' (王) means 'wàng' (旺), that is, 'magnificent, thriving'. [The English edition has the following for the two passages discussed: 'Straighten up your body, unify your vision, and the harmony of Heaven will come to you' (ibid.); 'man of kingly virtue' (ibid., p. 85).]

24 See Laozi, *Daodejing*, p. 87.
25 See Zhuangzi, *Complete Works*, pp. 109f.
26 See ibid., p. 7.
27 Ibid., p. 153.
28 See ibid., pp. 145–55 (section 19: 'Mastering Life').
29 See ibid., pp. 42–54 (section 6: 'The Great and Venerable Teacher').
30 Kleist, 'On the Marionette Theatre', p. 24.

Land and Sea – Strategies of Thinking

1 Antoine de Saint-Exupéry, *Citadelle*, in *Oeuvres complètes*, Vol. II, Paris: Gallimard, 1999, p. 680: 'Fonde l'amour des tours qui dominent les sables.' [The quotation is not contained in the English edition: *The Wisdom of the Sands*, New York: Harcourt, Brace and Company, 1950.]
2 Georg Wilhelm Friedrich Hegel, 'Konzept der Rede beim Antritt des philosophischen Lehramtes an der Universität Berlin (Einleitung zur Enzyklopädie-Vorlesung)', in *Enzyklopädie der philosophischen Wissenschaften III (Die Philosophie des Geistes)*, Werke, Vol. 10, Frankfurt am Main: Suhrkamp, 1986, pp. 399–417; here p. 416. [The German edition contains the draft of Hegel's inaugural lecture as an appendix; it is omitted in the English translation: *Philosophy of Mind*, trans. W. Wallace and A. V. Miller, Oxford: Clarendon, 2007.]
3 Georg Wilhelm Friedrich Hegel, *The Philosophy of History*, Kitchener: Batoche Books, 2001, p. 108.
4 Immanuel Kant, *Prolegomena to Any Future Metaphysics That Will Be Able to Come Forward as Science*, Cambridge: Cambridge University Press, 1997, pp. 11f.
5 Immanuel Kant, 'What is Orientation in Thinking?', in *Political Writings*, Cambridge: Cambridge University Press, 1991, pp. 237–49, here: p. 244.

6 Ibid., p. 241.

7 Ibid., p. 240 (emphasis added, B.-Ch. Han).

8 Martin Heidegger, 'Postscript to "What is Metaphysics?"', in *Pathmarks*, Cambridge: Cambridge University Press, 1998, pp. 231–90; here: p. 234.

9 Ibid., p. 233.

10 Heidegger, *Sojourns*, p. 48.

11 Martin Heidegger, *What Is Called Thinking?*, New York: Harper & Row, 1968, p. 192.

12 Martin Heidegger, *Mindfulness*, London: Continuum, 2006, p. 213 (transl. modified).

13 See Zhuangzi, *Complete Works*, p. 1.

14 See ibid., p. 2.

15 Ibid., p. 1.

16 Ibid., p. 6 [Except the conclusion, which the English edition renders: 'Little understanding cannot come up to great understanding' (ibid., p. 2).]

17 See Revelation 21:1: 'And I saw a new heaven and a new earth: for the first heaven and the first earth were passed away; and there was no more sea.' Apparently the idea that the sea's amorphous nature and depth symbolise a power that destroys God's solid order was common among both the Greeks and the Jews.

18 In *The Odyssey* it says: 'Now I will tell you all the old wizard's tricks . . . / First he will make his rounds and count the seals / and once he's checked their number, reviewed them all, / down in their midst he'll lie, like a shepherd with his flock. / That's your moment. Soon as you see him bedded down, / muster your heart and strength and hold him fast, / wildly as he writhes and fights you to escape. / He'll try all kinds of escape – twist and turn / into every beast that moves across the earth, / transforming himself into water, superhuman fire, / but you hold on for dear life, hug him all the harder! / And when, at last, he begins to ask questions – / back in the shape you saw him sleep at first – relax your grip and set the old god free / ask him outright hero, / which of the gods is up in arms against you? / How can you cross the swarming sea and reach home at last?' Homer, *The Odyssey*, New York: Viking, 1996, p. 137.

19 The Sirens call out to Odysseus: 'moor your ship on our coast so you can hear our song! / Never has any sailor passed our shores in his black craft / until he has heard the honeyed voices pouring from our lips, / and once he hears to his heart's content sails on, a wiser man. / . . . / all that comes to pass on the fertile earth, we know it all!' Ibid., p. 277.

20 Kant, *Critique of Judgment*, p. 103.

21 Ibid., p. 115.

22 Zhuangzi, *Complete Works*, p. 45.

23 Hegel, *The Philosophy of History*, p. 108.

24 Ibid.

25 Zhuangzi, *Complete Works*, p. 126.

26 Bashō, *Bashō's Haiku*, p. 47.

27 Laotse, *Daodejing*, p. 19.

28 Ibid., p. 161.

29 Zhuangzi, *Complete Works*, p. 128.

30 This state of undividedness is, however, not a state of chaos. The idea of chaos, or rather of the dichotomy between chaos and order, is alien to Chinese thinking.

31 See Zhuangzi, *Complete Works*, p. 59. [The English version renders 'Mitte', 'middle', as 'central region'.]

32 *The Ox and His Herdsman: A Chinese Zen Text. With commentary and Pointers by Master D. R. Otsu*, Tokyo: The Hokuseido Press, 1969, p. 20.

33 Transl. note: The German is '*in Welt sticht*', a play on the idiomatic expression 'in See stechen', which means 'to set sail', but literally translates as 'to stab into sea'.

34 Friedrich Nietzsche, *Nachgelassene Fragmente 1888–1889*, Kritische Gesamtausgabe, Vol. VIII.3, Berlin: De Gruyter, 1972, p. 44.

35 Friedrich Nietzsche, *Thus Spoke Zarathustra*, Cambridge: Cambridge University Press, 2006, p. 64.

36 Ibid., p. 186.

37 Ibid., p. 81.

38 Ibid., p. 192.

39 See e.g. ibid., pp. 179ff. and pp. 227ff.

40 Confucius, *Analects: With Selections from Traditional Commentaries*, Indianapolis: Hackett, 2003, p. 92.

41 Transl. note: My translation follows the German text. The English version has: 'I, however, am different from all of them in that I have no preconceived notions of what is permissible and what is not.' Ibid., p. 219.

42 Transl. note: I follow the German. Book 9 of Confucius's *Analects* is referenced, but I could not locate a corresponding passage.

43 Immanuel Kant, *Critique of Practical Reason*, Cambridge: Cambridge University Press, 2015, p. 130.

44 Ibid. Separation and distinction are probably the fundamental traits of Greek-Western thinking. The 'being' of Parmenides is a product of a separation (Greek: *krinein*): 'The goddess of Truth who guides Parmenides, puts two pathways before him, one of uncovering, one of hiding; but this signifies nothing else than that Dasein is already both in the truth and in untruth. The way of uncovering is achieved only in κρίυειυ λόγώ – in distinguishing between these understandingly, and making one's decision for the one rather than the other.' Martin Heidegger, *Being and Time*, Oxford: Blackwell, 1962, p. 265.

45 René Descartes, *Discourse on the Method*, in *Philosophical Writings*, Vol. 1, Cambridge: Cambridge University Press, 1985, pp. 111–51; here: p. 125.

46 René Descartes, *Principles of Philosophy*, in *Philosophical Writings*, Vol. 1, pp. 193–291; here: p. 240.

47 Roland Barthes, *Empire of Signs*, New York: The Noonday Press, 1989, p. 14.

Doing and Happening – Beyond Active and Passive
1 John Cage, '45' for a Speaker', in *Silence: Lectures and Writings*, Hanover: Wesleyan University Press, 1973, pp. 146–192; here: p. 191.

2 Yoshida Kenkō, *Essays in Idleness: The Tsuretsuregusa of Kenkō*, New York: Columbia University Press, 1967, p. 3. [A translation following the German version more closely would be: 'When alone and at leisure, I sit all day in front of my inkpot and write down whatever goes through my head, without coherence and without following a specific intention. I always feel quite quaint when doing this.']

3 See Martin Heidegger, *Time and Being*, New York: Harper & Row, 1972, p. 18: 'But what does this "It" mean? Philologists and philosophers of language have given the matter much thought without arriving at any valid clarification. The area of meaning meant by the It extends from the irrelevant to the demonic.' Heidegger apparently finds it hard to give up the figure of the subject. For him, the 'it' is a demonic super-subject that is still attached to the old structure of subjectivity.

4 Zhuangzi, *Complete Works*, p. 20.

5 See Bruno Lewin, *Abriß der japanischen Grammatik*, Wiesbaden: Harrassowitz Verlag, 1996.

6 Confucius, *The Analects*, p. 208.

7 Jacques Derrida, 'Violence and Metaphysics: An Essay on the Philosophy of Emmanuel Lévinas', in *Writing and Difference*, Chicago: University of Chicago Press, 1978, pp. 79–153, here: p. 147.

8 Georg Wilhelm Friedrich Hegel, *Hegel and the Human Spirit: A Translation of the Jena Lectures on the Philosophy of Spirit (1805/06)*, Detroit: Wayne State University Press, 1983, p. 87; for the phrases following the last ellipsis, see p. 87, n. 7 and n. 6.

9 Friedrich Nietzsche, *On the Genealogy of Morality*, Cambridge: Cambridge University Press, 2006, p. 26.

10 Bashō, *Bashō's Haiku*, p. 132.

11 Li Po, 'Mountain Dialogue', in *The Selected Poems of Li Po*, New York: New Directions, 1996, p. 32.

12 Martin Heidegger, *On the Way to Language*, New York: Harper & Row, 1971, p. 135.

13 Ibid., p. 108.

14 Martin Heidegger, *Off the Beaten Track*, Cambridge: Cambridge University Press, 2002 (preliminary remark).

15 Martin Heidegger, *Thought Poems: A Translation of Heidegger's Verse*, Lanham: Rowman & Littlefield, 2021, p. 575. – 'im Unzugangbaren sich versagende Ortschaft', Martin Heidegger, *Aus der Erfahrung des Denkens*, Gesamtausgabe I, Vol. 13, Frankfurt am Main: Klostermann, 1983, p. 223.

16 Heidegger speaks of 'the plight of wavering darkness in the waiting light', *Thought Poems*, p. 573. – 'Not zögernden

113

Dunkels im wartenden Licht', *Aus der Erfahrung des Denkens*, p. 222.
17 Martin Heidegger, *The Principle of Reason*, Indianapolis: Indiana University Press, 1991, p. 127.
18 *The Ox and His Herdsman*, p. 86.
19 Heidegger, *The Principle of Reason*, p. 68.
20 Ibid., p. 112 (transl. mod.).

Greeting and Bowing – Friendliness

1 Peter Handke, *Phantasien der Wiederholung*, Frankfurt am Main: Suhrkamp, 1983, p. 12.
2 Transl. note: The etymology of the English 'to greet' is related. In Old English *gretan* can mean 'to come in contact with', 'attack', as well as 'salute' or 'welcome'. And like the Old High German 'gruozen', it is derived from West Germanic *grotjan*.
3 *Etymologisches Wörterbuch des Deutschen*, Berlin: Akademie Verlag, 1989, Vol. 1. See also https://www.dwds.de/wb/etym wb/gr%C3%BC%C3%9Fen.
4 See Jochen Splett, *Althochdeutsches Wörterbuch*, Berlin and New York: De Gruyter, 1993, Vol. I.1.
5 Georg Wilhelm Friedrich Hegel, *Jenenser Realphilosophie*, Vol. 1, Leipzig: Felix Meiner, 1932, p. 227.
6 Martin Heidegger, *Hölderlin's Hymn 'Remembrance'*, Bloomington: Indiana University Press, 2018, p. 43 (German in brackets added).
7 Ibid.
8 Ibid., p. 44.
9 Ibid.
10 Ibid.
11 Ibid., p. 46.
12 Ibid., p. 43.
13 Barthes, *Empire of Signs*, p. 68.
14 Emmanuel Levinas, *Otherwise than Being or Beyond Essence*, Dordrecht: Springer, 1991, p. 85.
15 Transl. note: The terminology is Heideggerian. See the entry on 'Nothing (Nichts)' in *The Cambridge Heidegger Lexicon*, ed. Mark A. Wrathall, Cambridge: Cambridge University Press, 2021; pp. 520–28.

114

16 Wilhelm Gundert, the German translator of the *Bi-yan-lu*, rightly calls it the 'classic document of the first thriving Zen movement in Eastern Asia'.

17 Transl. note: My translation from the German version. The existing English translation reads: 'Yangshan asked Sansheng, "What's your name?" . . . Sansheng said, "Hug." . . . Yangshan said, "Hug? That's me." . . . Sansheng said, "My name is Huiran." . . . Yangshan laughed.' *The Blue Cliff Record*, p. 310.